Life with the Ojibwe

A Northern Land

Howard D. Paap

Badger Books Inc.
Oregon, Wis.

© Copyright 2001 by Howard D. Paap

Edited by Patrick Reardon
Published by Badger Books Inc.
Illustrations by Keller Paap

First edition

ISBN 1-878569-78-3

Badger Books Inc.
P.O. Box 192
Oregon, WI 53575
Toll-free phone: (800) 928-2372
Web site: http://www.badgerbooks.com
E-Mail: books@badgerbooks.com

This book is dedicated to Marlene, the love of my life.

Whatever evaluation we finally make about a stretch of land,...no matter how profound or accurate, we will find it inadequate. The land retains an identity of its own, still deeper and more subtle than we can know. Our obligation toward it then becomes simple: to approach with an uncalculating mind, with an attitude of regard. To try to sense the range and variety of its expression—its weather and colors and animals. To intend from the beginning to preserve some of the mystery within it as a kind of wisdom to be expressed, not questioned. And to be alert for its openings, for that moment when something sacred reveals itself within the mundane, and you know the land knows you are there.

— **Barry Lopez,** *Arctic Dreams*

Acknowledgments

Many, many people—as well as other forms of existence—were involved in the creation of this book. First of all, the *Anishinaabeg* are recognized, those at Red Cliff today, certainly, but also all of those in the past that I was too late to get to know. And all those hunters and gatherers of the very distant past are involved in this manuscript as well. They were the pioneers; they set the stage, hundreds and even thousands of years ago. I particularly acknowledge those of the 1700's, 1800's and mid-1900's at Red Cliff.

To all the people mentioned in this book, whether by using real names or fictitious ones, I am indebted.

Badger Books of Oregon, Wisconsin, and editor and publisher Marv Balousek are acknowledged for their decision that this manuscript was worthwhile and warranted publishing.

For reading the manuscript before publication and suggesting changes, I thank Delores Bainbridge, Ron DePerry, Patricia Basina Deperry, Chuck Basina, Lynn Basina and Ruby Basina. For creating the lined drawings, I thank Keller DePerry Augustine Paap.

And for being part of all this, I thank my wife, Marlene. Her quiet support is constant. Our children and their spouses have been integral also, and thanks go out to them as well: Max and Sue, Beth and Scott, Keller and Lisa. And thanks to our grandchildren: Mijen, Grace, Elsa and Binesi. A special thanks goes to Gladys Angeline Roy-DePerry for her patience with a sometimes too-loud son-in-law.

A *chi-miigwech* to all!

— Howard D. Paap

Contents

Acknowledgments 7

Prologue 11

The Comfort of Woods 17

Trapping with Tom 33

The Progressive Dinner 49

A Need for Paint 59

Tobacco on the Water 71

The Flowers of Red Cliff 93

Holding Court 107

Pageantry 121

Repatriation 129

Red Clay 139

Pow wows 155

Empty Nets 169

Joe Attikoosh 181

A Woodland Artistry 197

Night Forest 207

A Shoreline Dream 223

Prologue

For the past forty years I have been able to spend time with the land and people of the Red Cliff Indian Reservation in far Northern Wisconsin. These years have been a major part of my life. Much has changed over these four decades, both with the community of Red Cliff and also with me. Initially I went to the community as a young military veteran turned college student searching for the pathway I would make for the rest of my years. Little did I know then how important Red Cliff would become to me.

With the passing of so many years, it is hoped, would come wisdom. The people of Red Cliff can decide for themselves whether or not I have learned anything. Since first coming to the community I have spent over thirty years studying and teaching the academic discipline of anthropology. Also, in the interim I have enjoyed forty years of marriage, enjoyed watching our children grow and leave home, and now am deeply enmeshed in the joy of grandchildren. The time has come for a summing-up. Is it wise to do so?

While my times at Red Cliff have often been driven by intellectual curiosity, they have more importantly been times of deep and intimate personal involvement. Does this personal tie mean I should not write about the community? Would it be best to not tell my story—best to leave it alone? For decade after decade I have tried to do so. But now, obviously, I have chosen to write; after all, it is my story, my interpretation. Furthermore, there is too much at stake here—first to appease a tired old ego with its never resting contemplative mind that says there are still far too many questions that beg for resolution. Too much learning still needs to be done, and while someone reared in the oral tradition can, it seems, be content to let it all be unwritten, the reader needs to know that I was reared in the literate tradition. A deep urging inside me causes me to write. Some of the biases I carry are from many of the classroom teachers I encountered through the years. These educators and scholars not only insisted that I learn what they taught, but that I also write it down.

Perhaps writing is really all about the ego. Perhaps we writers, however naive, feel that sometime, somewhere, someone might pick up our scribblings and not only find them amusing, and thus, the reader, if not actually informed, might in some small way be comforted by them.

My second reason for writing is that I hear a strong, growing voice asking about Red Cliff and many other communities like it. More and more Red Cliff people are thinking about the past of their community, its present and future. They are told the old stories by the Elders as well as the new stories that keep coming with the years. And now with the relative ease of recording these electronically, we should expect to see more writing being done. But interestingly, this new trend of looking to the literature is growing at Red Cliff right along with the old desire to let it all be unwritten. Despite what has been said and written about Red Cliff, it is a traditional Ojibwe community. I am beginning to realize that it has always been this way. Hopefully this growth of both the old and new will continue. These two trends are not mutually exclusive.

By writing I hope to speak to that voice asking about the community, but I also hope to speak to that voice reminding me of the strong taboo against writing about certain subjects. In this manuscript I hope I have honored the pleas of both these voices. There are matters that must not be written except in the heart. A people's identity is their own business and we must understand that just as there are some things better left unsaid, there are some things better left unwritten.

While much of the history of Red Cliff has been told, it is yet to be written. This collection of essays provides an accounting of one person's selected experiences in the community. In a small way it might stand as another addition to a much longer and richer history of the place that is Red Cliff. At base, these essays are a statement about the land. The reader needs to know that Red Cliff has both a space/time dimension (a geography, i.e., location, and a history) and a human dimension, (a people). And always, as the early Ojibwe ethnologist A.I. Hallowell saw, there are "other-than-human" persons as well. These are the *manidoog* that for time immemorial are part of Ojibwe communities. Like the people, they live with the earth, water and sky. Together, the spirits, people, land, water and sky interact to achieve *pimadaziwin*—the old Ojibwe word sometimes translated, minimally, as "The Good Life."

In the following essays I have told of experiences of mine at Red Cliff. These events occurred in the community's space and time, and they involved some of the community's persons— both human and nonhuman. All the events actually occurred, but out of respect some of the names have been changed. If there are errors of interpretation then I eagerly await discussions about them. If there are errors of fact, they are mine and mine alone. In this latter case, I eagerly welcome their correction.

Anthropology teaches you to participate while observing. The anthropologist must always try to be part of the community under study, but also must stand aside to watch and listen. For years I told my students that while I agree with this dictum, I also felt it was impossible, as the pioneering anthropologist Bronislaw Malinowski admonished us, to "be a participant-observer." This old field technique is meant to bring objectivity. Yet, always the field worker should recognize that the maintenance of a neutral objectivity is an ideal that is never really achieved. All that can be done is to try.

This is not just a book about a small Indian reservation. It is meant to make a statement about other communities as well, especially those that people like the Ojibwe have had to deal with in order to survive. However Red Cliff is characterized, we need to understand that it is communities like this that have had to become expert on multi-culturalism, cultural and racial diversity, the politics of power, and the other concepts and initiatives currently being articulated in what is sometimes called "the greater society." Red Cliff does not have to be taught these concepts. Its leaders have been using their underlying principles for generations. Right from the first encounters with the Europeans, perhaps back in the early 1600's, the forbears of the community have manipulated these concepts in order to survive. Thus, this book offers a story about a world larger than Red Cliff.

The Comfort of Woods

When we destroy the environment we are destroying ourselves.
— **Peter Mathiesson-1999**

I've just awakened from a night of sound sleep. The cabin was cozy-warm when I turned in a few hours after sundown, but now it's chilly and I don't wait to pull on my jeans before starting a fire. Yesterday's labor must have been especially exhausting because I slept through the night without rising to stuff firewood into the stove.

It's still dark but I'm eager to get into the day. I light the glass oil lamp, then place a few slivers of cedar kindling on the remaining hot coals buried in the stove's ashes, go to the pile of large dry white birch and ash on the floor behind the cabin's front door. I carefully but quickly place a few pieces in the stove on top of the crackling cedar. Reaching for my cold jeans I hold them above the stove for a moment, hoping to warm them, but the fire does not yet throw heat. I slip into the jeans, then find my flannel shirt and button it on. For several cold moments I crowd next to the aging and dented barrel stove that sits squarely in the center of the cabin floor. Finally my open palms feel the first faint waves of emanating heat.

It's March. I'm on the Red Cliff Indian Reservation, at the very tip of the mainland of Northern Wisconsin, only a few hundred yards from Lake Superior. I can't hear the lake because of its ice cover that clamps the waves tight, nor can I see it even in daylight, because of the surrounding tall hard maples. I'm in a sugarbush. It's another time of teaching and learning, only here I am the student.

The sugarbush's trees are part of the eighteen miles of wooded shoreline that make up the reservation. Like a fingernail at the edge of the Bayfield Peninsula, it overlooks Lake Superior and its Apostle Islands. A high, rough land, creased with deep ravines washing to the lake, the reservation is a place of tough red clay, red sandstone outcrops and boggy lowlands. Oaks, maples, ashes, birches, aspens and an array of conifers make up these dense woods.

For the past two weeks I've been working at hauling white and yellow rounds from the ridge behind the cabin to the boiling site. The chunks are lifted onto a homemade tin-bottomed wooden sled, the sort used in this camp for generations, then pulled and pushed to the boiling kettles. Hours each day were spent raising a six-pound steel maul over the larger, more twisted pieces, and a sharp double-bitted axe over the easier split smaller ones, rendering them asunder with directed blows. Amidst this firewood making came the hauling of sap, the tending of the fire. It is a tradition to work hard here. Those who do not are jokingly chastised and after a day or two leave camp for the comforts of the reservation village.

With a little imagination, I envision the camp's cedar log cabin fitting between the trees like a tiny hut in some mythical forest, sketched onto a page in a book of fairy tales. The storybook shows a dark, primeval forest with the cabin's windows beaming golden light into the night. This morning, I see darkness looking back at me when I glance at a window. Except for the white-bellied woods mouse that shares this cabin with me, I am alone.

Suddenly I hear the welcome song of a lone robin heralding the hint of light that will soon diffuse through the eastern treetops. An early arriving forest robin. I go to the door and search the sky above the trees, but see no light. How does the bird know? It either has much better eyesight than I, or has a sixth sense. Once again, I ponder the easy behavior of the others.

Impatient, like the bird, I do not wait for the wood burning fire to boil water. Instead, I turn on the propane range and hurriedly heat yesterday's coffee. Then, after a sip of the bitter, black espresso-like remains from yesterday, I dump the thick mess outside and start a new pot. A fresh new day deserves fresh coffee.

There is a hushed compactness in this dark morning. The night does not want to leave, despite the robin's song. It crowds in around the cabin, comes through the closed windows and doors, and pushes against the slowly flickering oil lamp. These brief moments, when he last of night trysts with the first of day, are special. At these times, I move from dark to light.

Being alone in these shoreline woods allows opportunity for their contemplation. In a surging spate of self-pity—or real-ism—I identify with these woods, feel I can imagine their world as they live it. After a near lifetime of work I sometimes feel buffered and battered as I imagine the trees do.

A second generation German-American, coming from a line of immigrant workers, peasants really, I still see and feel the big-handed greetings from now-dead uncles at family reunions in far, southern Wisconsin. We were farmers. In important ways I still am one.

We knew the land, felt it, although we thought little of whose it was before we came to claim it, to make it ours with our plows. We pulled stumps, drained swamps, picked rocks. We were doing what the country asked us to. We produced food for the new masses, for those in cities. And in the process we tamed the countryside, made it over. The arrow points we oc-casionally found in our spring fields were kept in wooden cigar boxes on closet shelves. Some were wired onto hardboard, framed and displayed in dusty county museums. They shared space with huge thin sliced rounds of trees that marked the rings, the times of the past.

In this sugarbush I think of all that. I look at these trees and conclude that they too have been asked to give themselves for the "development" of "this great nation," laying throughout the reservation, like decaying tombstones. They and their ancestors have been hacked at, slashed and cut for over a hundred years. Signs of their exploitation and extraction are everywhere for the watchful eye and open mind. Like decaying tombstones, crumbling monster white pine and hemlock stumps, their decaying tentacles still grasping the earth in a death embrace, lay throughout the reservation. Bent and misshapen hardwoods, left as deformed, passed up by the last wave of loggers, reach, gaspingly for sunlight. Everywhere the younger balsam fir and hemlocks, now usually considered to be waste or "trash" trees, try to gain a foothold, to grab some light.

Scattered amidst these species, especially in lower areas, are the white cedars. A special tree, a sacred tree, the cedar is the axis mundi of Ojibwe religious ideology. As such, these fragrant trees catch my eye and hold it. They command attention. Their presence permeates these woods.

In a few places remnants of barbed wire can be seen embedded in bulging tree trunks. These old fence lines, attempts at containment, were finally overwhelmed by the ongoing life of the trees themselves. Layer after layer of new growth literally swallowed, ate up, these metal tools of the last century's distant lawmakers, who, while sitting in their Washington chairs, decreed that the Ojibwe of Red Cliff must become farmers. And farmers need fences, need notions of properties.

So, clearings were made for potatoes, turnips, rutabagas, hay and grains. Today, if the onlooker knows where to look some can still be detected. These "fields" are as faint as old, long unused logging trails.

The woods still show faint evidence of these trails, pathways slashed over hill and across ravine, first for the steel-shoed hooves of heavily muscled draft horses, then for gasoline driven machines. The oldest now grown over, it is the newer ones that tell of the harshness of the taking. Bulldozer blades leave piles of earth, stone, and broken, torn wood, all pushed aside, out of the way. Now and then a broken copper boiler can be spotted, often reaching up from the earth, partly buried by passing time. Hard steel rings of galvanized buckets are found, their thinner steel long disintegrated, returned from whence it came. These are the remnants of battle. The eastern people came, cutting their way, then leaving. Now the woods stand, healing until the next surge, the next harvest. But these trees keep coming back. The Red Cliff Ojibwe have their own history of "harvesting" the same trees. In the very late 1800's and early 1900's, the tribesmen were often the yielders of the sharp axe and saw. They, like the new Easterners, felled the trees, reduced them to lumber. Small scale loggers—tribal members—subsisted in this business into the middle of the 1900's at Red Cliff. Today, logging with the involvement of the Bureau of Indian Affairs, still goes on.

The Indian logging of a hundred years ago is, perhaps, troubling, and needs to be placed into the context of the times. Under extreme duress, with pressures to assimilate into the mainstream, the tribal people often had no other choice. Indians were deemed to be vanishing. Manifest Destiny was a powerful god. Hunting and fishing were not what they were earlier, and were placed under the control of downstate lawmakers. They were scheduled into seasons, if not actually outlawed entirely. The priests and nuns, the school officials all said it had to come—the change.

The trees were sawed into lumber that framed the wooden structures of cities like Chicago, and later further west to South Dakota and elsewhere. These reservation lands were stripped, left in such a disarray that at the turn of the twentieth century an Indian agent said they were uninhabitable. But uninhabitable or not, the Ojibwe stayed as their forest started the process of healing. So, today the woods and its people remain, still recovering, in some places still in trauma, but nevertheless healing until the next surge, the next harvest.

Now warmed, with a heavy ceramic cup of fresh, hot, tasty coffee, I arm my way into my camp jacket, pull on my woolen toque, and leave the cabin to enjoy the first hint of daylight. I walk out into the camp's clearing and pause beside the wood pile. Here I stand to sip the coffee, to watch and listen.

With the coming of light I notice, at my feet, in a patch of bare ground where the spring sun has melted the snow, two ankle high seedlings of white pine, germinated from a rare larger seed tree a hundred feet away. The little green trees, struggling for a toehold among the golden thread and wintergreen plants on the forest floor, are a pleasure to see. It was the white pines that first drew the lumber cutters, buyers, dealers. How vulnerable these little pines! How vulnerable this entire forest!

Yet, these trees tell of strength, of endurance. They are still here. They draw up earth's water, spread their boughs out into the air, and produce seed. The seed falls, nestles into the earth, sprouts and takes root. A new tree appears. This persistence is heartening to me. These tiny pines, with the sugarbush's hard maples, and all their other companions, are like the others of the forest — the four-leggeds, the winged and furried ones, like those who live in the waters. They are like the *migisiwag* and *ma'iinganag* — the bald eagles and timber wolves — who have recently returned to the reservation after decades of absence. And, importantly, they are like the *Anishinaabeg* who run this camp.

My childhood and youth were spent in Wisconsin. All that time I never pondered the meaning of the word. Through the years of elementary, secondary and even college education, it was never defined. Wisconsin was just another "Indian" word. Our map was dotted with rivers, counties, and towns with such old names. We paid them no heed, except perhaps, as at Thanksgiving, when we might conjure images of dark skinned people with feathers in their hair. In my family, in my often frantic, unthinking life, the question of the word's meaning, of its necessary referent, was never raised. We did not ponder such things.

Since then I have learned Wisconsin is an Anishinaabe word. It is sometimes translated as "inside the small beaver lodge."

Here in the Northwoods this definition is borne out. It has been five days now since I've had a bath. I feel like a musky animal slowly waking inside my darkened lodge, while outside the departing night, with its crowding trees, pushes against my walls for one last embrace. It is time for spring.

Here, winter seems as long as summer. The dark time of cold is counterpoised to the time of warmth and light. Spring and fall can be but glimpses of an exuberant paradise, fleeting windows of eternity between the two bigger seasons. The slow rhythms of these seasons flow inside us with a presence as sure as the beating of our hearts. Summer's few hot, humid days stand with winter's fierce cold and together create a pulsating tension deep inside us. In this rural countryside we meld with the seasons.

The snow can carpet the forest with a pile several feet thick. When the temperatures drop to thirty or forty below there is little activity. Machines often stop, and both humans and animals burrow deep to stay the course. At such times even the ravens stay put. Yet, in a paradoxical way, the snow is an insulator. It crowds up to us, like a welcome bed partner and, despite its chill, can warm our bodies and minds. In Northern Wisconsin you learn to live with snow and cold.

I come to the woods to escape the crowds of the suburbs. I replace the people with trees. For years I have labored with my mind in urban places. My occupation as a teacher deals with abstractions that cannot speak to the whole of my human needs. So each spring, for a few weeks, here in the forest, my mind relaxes while my muscles go to work. The labor I offer in my friends' sugarbush is strenuous, but it brings a welcome fatigue. The maples and I have survived another winter, and together we celebrate. While winter's cold withdraws, the rising sap is caught and boiled over a hot hardwood fire, then condensed to a vernal sweetness. Spring is sweet in the sugarbush.

Maple syrup is a given on the menu out here. A Mason jar sits on the table beside the unrefrigerated plastic ketchup bottle and the can of peanut butter. Instead of milk, I eat the fresh, dark and smoky syrup on my oatmeal.

This is a thick place. These woods have not been logged for over fifty years. The mature maples can be four feet or more in diameter at their bases. The white birches and yellow aspens that are scattered amongst them are tall, their branches forming only well up in the canopy. The lower space is often filled with dark green balsams, hemlocks and white cedar trees that live scattered throughout these hardwoods. These needled conifers form a dark, emerald wall, impossible to see through.

We truly are short sighted here. The only way to see the horizon is to walk to the big lake. I sometimes strap on my snowshoes to follow the game trail that leads through the trees. Upon reaching the high red banks, now white with snow, the world opens up again as I lift my eyes to the distant white horizon line between the snow-covered ice and the sky. Sand Island and Raspberry Island, two of the westernmost Apostles, sit like frozen, isolated dark groves, out on the ice.

People who live year-round in these northern forested places lose sight of distances. They are not good map readers. It's as if they plot their courses from tree to tree. There is a present orientation here. You cannot see great distances so you must deal with the facts at hand.

I once asked a local resident what it was about Northern Wisconsin that appealed to him. "I don't have to drive miles and miles to get to it," he replied. "It's here, right before me, no matter where I am."

This immediacy is reflected in the speech of the longtime residents. Conversations get to the point, and any lengthy analysis is carried on internally, with silent monologues. Understatement is the vogue, as if there is little to say about what should be obvious. In one small community if you ask who was seen in town, a person might reply with, "John and 'dem," leaving the listener to conclude who the "'dem" are.

Like the trees themselves, there is a steadfastness about people who live in these northern forests. Those who stay remind you of families in houses at the ends of country roads. They have chosen their spots and have settled in for the duration. There is often only one way out and that is south, "down the line," to the open spaces of central and southern Wisconsin. The cold vastness of Lake Superior blocks any further passage north.

A brother-in-law once gave me a road atlas for a Christmas gift. At a time in my life when I was regularly flying off to conferences in distant places, it was a message that recognized my life as different from his. After a youthful stint in the military, he came home and stayed put. A book of maps, with their maze of red, blue and black lines on page after page was his way of saying who I was—and who he is.

These woods are "Up North," and the rest of the state is "down," as if you were speaking about poles on a vertical dimension. There is little horizontal movement here. It's not like life on the plains and prairies where roads meet at intersections at regular intervals and point to the cardinal directions.

Once, when driving from Superior eastward to Ashland, an unusual sensation of "glancing off" came to me. It was a feeling of obliqueness. There is a welcome strangeness about travelling Highway 2 along this route. When on this road you move horizontally, ignoring the pull of the north-south axis. You skirt the often common, even frenzied rush of life to and from the state's more southern cities.

Roads seem to end here. This notion of terminus is reflected in the speech of residents who, when greeting a visitor ask, "Where'd ya come from?" rather than "Where you going?" The question says that the visitor has arrived. There is no further place to go. This is the end of the trail. This is the destination.

Today will be another bright day. The sun will slowly climb and the sap will be pulled up from its nightly sanctuaries in the tree roots. The cool west wind, almost constant during daylight hours through much of March, will be heard high in the tree tops. Black-capped chickadees will come in to the camp, welcoming us with their twittering as they flit from tree to tree.

Nestled in the snow, the low cabin will be safe from the

wind. These longer, warmer days of the approaching spring
have crusted the snow. Now when I walk on the trails from tree
to tree to collect the sap, I walk high. It's a heady experience,
almost mystical, to be up out of your usual place, levitating on
the hardened snow. The internal tension of being weighted down
with buckets of clear, sweet maple sap, while at the same time,
moving up in a high place, is compelling. When hauling sap I
balance between two worlds.

Once, in a fit of madness, I drank a large measure of sap
right from the bucket. There was a lull in the day's work and
while a companion tended the boiling kettles, I wandered off
into the woods, up to the edge of the dark hemlock grove where
the Virginia deer yard-up for winter.

I was on a small rise that allowed me to gaze down upon the
cabin, the huge pile of firewood, and the wall-less boiling shed.
The smoke from the fire and the steam from the boiling kettles
mingled with a light morning fog that still lay in the hollow. I
took a bucket off a nearby tree, tipped it to my lips and drank a
long measure. Raw, natural maple sap, cold as ice, flowed down
my throat into my warm stomach. This joyful polar collapse,
this coming together of warmth and cold, of winter and spring,
takes place each March in the sugarbush.

This sugarbush has been operated by tribal members for over
one hundred and fifty years, and perhaps longer. Stories are
told of the times before the cedar cabin was built. Then a small
slant roofed wooden board shed, covered with tarpaper was where
the camp workers slept, cooked their meals, and gathered to
keep warm on the coldest days. Before the shed, which now
serves to store sap cans and other tools in the off season, different makeshift structures sufficed. Most were made of poles and
birch bark. Some were conical, like teepees, otheres were ob-
long, like wigwams. Some were much smaller, in the shape of
low two-person canvas tents. All such early structures were minimal, but very substantial. Like this cedar cabin, the trees gave
the people shelter, protection.

This morning, ending my reverie at the woodpile, I stepped back into the cabin to boil oatmeal and enjoy the barrel stove's heat. I tried to recall how the camp looked before the building of the cabin. I remembered that fall in 1962 when my wife and I walked the two miles along the narrow footpath through the woods to get to the site. We had driven the seven miles out on the reservation's dirt roads, and parked our car at the trail head. An older cousin of my wife, Sam Newago, was working with the cedar logs he and his family cut the year before. We sat with him and ate the sandwiches we brought along. It was a colorful October afternoon. The slight bitterness of the hot green tea Sam served gently bit our tongues.

That was over thirty years ago. I concluded the camp has not changed much in the passing years. Sam was gone. Mike, his older brother, was struggling with health problems that made it increasingly difficult to get out to the sugarbush. Now the work was overseen by the next generation, by the sons of Sam and Mike.

In earlier times the sugarbush was run by the women. They saw to the tapping of trees, the hauling of sap and its boiling. Now a woman is rarely seen in camp. However, last Saturday, a family member, at age 68, walked in to cook a meal for us. I stood back and watched, thrilled as she moved about, taking charge of the afternoon. It was clear she knew how to run things. Although she busied herself inside the cabin with food preparation, at times she came out onto the small porch to sit in the warm sunlight. She was clearly at peace. We conversed easily. She patiently answered my questions, her statements highlighted with gentle laughter.

We men, three of us, who had been working the camp all week, were grateful for the cooked meal. Boiled potatoes with venison and its dark brown gravy were a delight. She even brought wild rice, quickly cooked it, and scooped it onto our plates. There was hot, fried bread that we dipped in maple syrup. We feasted. Later, as we drank cups of hot balsam tea, she said that "long ago" she used to come to the camp each year, and did most of the work herself.

She reminisced about years past — how, as a child, she spent days in camp with her grandparents. At times, she lapsed into silence, not wanting, I thought, to be spoken to. In these moments, she was gone from me, still here in camp, but with those of the earlier times, visiting with the elders, recalling the good times.

It was a good morning for musing, but soon I would hear the shouts of one of the Newago boys back on the trail. He would come to help with the sap hauling, and boiling. I liked to have the fire started before his arrival, so I put the coffee cup down, slipped into my tall rubber boots, and went outside.

Four thirty-gallon barrels of sap hung over the fire pit. It was from yesterday's hauling. I placed cedar kindling beneath them, stuffed in a sheet of newspaper from the cabin, and stood back to watch the flames catch. Then I piled the larger chunks of split yellow birch and ash around the cedar under the large kettles. The fire would have to be tended through the day. If kept hot enough, the sap could be finished late in the afternoon, turned into a deep, brown syrup.

I stood back to watch the new fire, then confident it was all right, I walked the fifteen yards or so out on a trail to the nearest maple tree. Not yet warmed by the sun to the point of allowing the sap to flow, the spout still held its little icicle of sap from last evening when it stopped running.

In the early morning silence, broken only by the crackling of the new boiling fire, the tall tree stood with its companions, waiting for another busy day. I reached into my shirt pocket, withdrew the folded package of Half and Half, opened it, and, inserting two fingers, withdrew a large pinch. I placed it on the ground at the base of the tree. Rising, I slowly gazed at the others, as I turned around to view the woods and, thankfully, acknowledge the start of another day. Except for the loud snaps and pops of the pieces of burning cedar there were no sounds.

A century and more ago the Europeans and new Americans called woods like these a desert. Not able to understand landscapes lacking, they thought, a human presence, they considered such forests wastelands. The trees were patiently awaiting the bite of the woodsman's axe. Once the trees were removed, the stumps burned, pulled or dynamited out, the earth was felt to be ready for the liberation of the plow's slicing cut.

The soil was turned over, the wooded landscape made to disappear. This was thought to be the will of the European's god. Manifest Destiny, an event destined to occur. It was manifest, so plainly clear, that those who dared to question it were ignored. The historical contradiction in the new country's penchant for clearing the forests, to fill these "empty" spaces, can be, to some, breath stopping. Its arrogance can be numbing. The Euro-Americans, those new people, knew they were right.

Northern Wisconsin's forests were deemed to be an empty wilderness. Ominously, today's calls for economic "development" of the northland, hauntingly ring with the unquestioning certainty of national voices of long ago. Today we are told that people need jobs, weekend, summer, and retirement homes, places to recreate. As in Canada, leaders look to the north, to what they consider "undeveloped" lands, for relief.

Today, the great ogre called "Development" is revisiting these Red Cliff woods. The ethic of material accumulation that inflicts the larger national society brings it back now and then. As I gaze at these strong trees, I wonder if they can withstand the latest "coming," this latest onslaught.

Along with troubling discussions of how the natural world was perceived by the country's Eastern newcomers, history's archives tell an even more humanly personal story. This issue constituted the question of just what criteria had to be present before human beings could be classified as "Men." In the latter decades of the 1800's, some societal leaders still felt that the humans who were found to be populating the forests, upon the arrival of the European, were not Men. This thinking harked back to the times of colonization on the Eastern Seaboard, when extreme voices suggested the tribesmen were not human beings, and, therefore, could be used for any purpose, even exterminated. Usually it was assumed they were not humans because they did not possess reason. Seen as a quality rather than a process, reason was held by Europeans, and a few others, but not by the New World's "savages." Unable to see that reason always lies in a bed of cultural assumptions, these early philosophers were certain that only "true Men" held reason. "Savages" did not.

In those earlier times more reasonable voices admitted that "the dusky Savages" were, indeed, humans and capable of being civilized. But it is striking that in the 1830's, and onward into the later decades of the 1800's, people like the French geologist, Joseph Nicolet and the Austrian missionary, Frederick Baraga, both who came among the Ojibwe of Madeline Island and Chequamegon Bay—populations from whence the community of Red Cliff was formed—still said it was impossible to turn them into Men. This begs the question of what Nicolet and Baraga meant by Men. But their meaning is clear. Men were people who were Christian, successfully engaged in the market exchange system evident at the time. Men were civilized.

Struggling with their perceptions of the New World, the early non-tribal Americans, the immigrants from the East could only interpret their "discovery" through their knowledge at the time. We do the same. We filter our experiences, give them meaning through our culturally constructed words. We must be careful.

This is what these trees do to me. Their power is strong. Their silent endurance causes self reflection. People have lost their minds in woods. No wonder, for in these places of extended solitude you must finally deal with yourself, with your community, your understandings.

My tobacco offering is so feeble. There must be more. Ceremonies and rituals can be overdone, executed routinely. In their comforting beauty, they might allow for the suspension of our personal responsibility.

This morning, in all the reassuring quietude offered by these trees, I still feel uneasy. It is as if the trees are questioning me. The gentle murmur in their tops that will rise in an hour or two, their sisagwad, as the past Ojibwe elder and writer, Ignatia Broker told us, wants to be heard. Will we listen? Will their question be registered?

Condo builders are coveting this wooded shoreline at Red Cliff. They are at the reservation's western boundaries, its southern boundaries, and in the case of Raspberry Point and the Red Cliff Creek area, in the community's very midst. Once again the speculators are here. And yesterday I learned that the outsider who "owns" the eighty acres of hardwoods, through which the first mile of the trail into this sugarbush runs, plans to log that land, to clear-cut it. This could be devastating to this camp, could change its secluded character for fifty years or so.

So I look to this woods and wonder what will be its future. I struggle to make sense of it all.

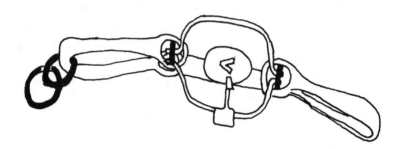

Trapping with Tom

The forests have never failed the Ojibway.
— Ignatia Broke, 1983

It's not clear to me if Tom always intended I join him that late March white winter day. Perhaps our trip was something that just happened. Either way—planned or not—it was a time of teaching. Now that Tom has been gone for a few years and I have had ample time to rethink our times together, I look upon him as one of my teachers, an instructor who taught more by his actions, and by his silence, than by spoken words. That March morning was the end of another sugarbush season for me. I had to return to the city. Spring term was starting Monday and I needed to be in the lecture hall, on line. My two weeks in the woods were over.

Winter's sublime wonder—the marvel of snow, of biting cold, of night skies awash with pastel Northern Lights that, some Ojibwe say, are the spirits of those who have gone beyond—had done its best to calm me, to set me a-right again. The waiting woods, its trees allowing me to take portions of their "life blood," to boil it to syrup, had been welcoming in its quietude. The Red Cliff wooded shoreline offered me another season of sugar making but, there was more in that quiet gesture.

The trees told me, again, of both the fragility of life, of its vulnerabilities, and of its persistence. Despite contemporary onslaughts of tourists in the forms of kayakers, casino gamblers, weekend cottage renters, snowmobilers, adventure-seeking dog

mushers, upscale sailboaters, hikers and others who come to the
reservation in increasing throngs, the woods and shoreline were
still here.

These trees, like Tom, are teachers. Conventional teaching,
that found in what we call our educational systems, is institu-
tionalized with its accompanying rules and guidelines. Its cur-
ricula, sometimes mandated by people sitting on "high level"
boards, are goal driven, standardized. Planned teaching, by its
nature, has a large element of expectation. There is foresight,
preparation and the formation of goals. All this can be burdened with cumbersome structure and anticipation. The joy of
spontaneous discovery can be quieted or, worse yet, not even
given a chance to emerge.

Tom's teaching may have been planned, but if so it was deliv-
ered with subtlety, with a very soft, quiet touch. His teachings,
to use that word Ojibwe traditionalists prefer, were often meant
to be pondered internally, to be contemplated over time. He
used no "lesson plans," and if he used a script it was an old one,
used by his parents and grandparents, and those who came before. His teachings came from inside him, from years of living,
of surviving, of accepting the reservation's woods, its Others,
the seasons, winds, the earth itself.

Tom walked into camp late Friday afternoon, helped me haul
sap and tend the last of the day's boiling. He stayed the night,
taking his usual cot in a cabin corner. After a week of nights
spent alone it was good to have his company. We sat up late, by
the oil lamp at the table, in conversation. Our voices were low,
like the murmur of flames we heard consuming the dry wood
in the barrel stove only feet away.

We talked, almost in hushed tones, I feel, because of the
quiet cabin and its surrounding woods. The presence of the
trees, outside in the darkness, was calming. But we also spoke
quietly because we were listening. It was a time of owls. All
week they called in the early of night, beside the cabin and up
on the ridge. When I made my daily journal entries just before

turning in, I wrote of them.

Throughout much of Native America country, the owl is presented as a harbinger of bad times, of death. Sometimes interpreted as a sign, an owl's call is not always welcomed. Yet, in the wonder of paradox, in Ojibwe legend the owl is a bringer of *medicine,* of power, of a quality sought after by the people. In these cases the owl is a helper, a *manidoo* that works for the people in good, welcome ways.

So to the Ojibwe, the owl, in its complexities, in its wonderment, brings both life and death. It had better be listened to. It has something to say. That Friday night Tom and I listened to the owls with evident pleasure, but without mentioning them. It was clear their calls brought us joy, but we did not bring it to voice except to comment briefly on the national issue in the news that week. That afternoon when Tom appeared in camp he brought the day's Ashland newspaper, and handed it to me saying, "Here, I know you like to keep up on the news."

This was a little joke between us because he knew my time spent in the sugarbush was a joy of solitude for me, a time of turning my back on the Evening News. Like others on the reservation who chose to, as much as was practicable, live off the land, many of his lifetime's hours had been spent alone, out on the big lake or in the woods. Yet, like most Ojibwe, he was very gregarious, enjoying the company of others. As is the custom, he did not dwell on this, did not choose to discuss it in lengthy discourses. His times of solitude were just part of his existence. They were left at that.

He also knew I was pleased with the absence of a mirror in the cabin, how this allowed me not to see anyone, even myself, when, as sometimes happened, I was alone two or three days at a time. Sometimes he told me to be sure to close my eyes when I took a bucket to the reflecting pool of runoff water that collected in the roots of a large maple nearby. We used this clean water to wash our few dishes and for taking sporadic sponge baths.

So his bringing the paper was a challenge, a way to test my

resolve to be alone, to leave the city behind. To him the paper was another teaching tool. He delighted in catching me in a weak moment when I'd sit at the table, reading it. That Friday's paper told, on the front page, how the diminutive spotted owl was holding up the logging of old growth forest in a western state. When I mentioned this to Tom he replied simply, "Yah, that little feller is raising hell. Good for him." That exchange was our extent of speaking of owls.

My bus was leaving Ashland early Sunday morning. After breakfast, I packed up, rolled my sleeping bag, and said my personal goodbyes to the sugarbush for another year. We had a few gallons of syrup to carry out so we tied them, with my gear, onto the camp's homemade tin-botttomed sled. I walked ahead, both arms behind me, pulling the sled's rope while Tom walked behind, pushing on the waist high two-by-four crossbar handle. The trail is just under two miles and with a few rises, so the walk always takes some time.

After about twenty minutes of plodding along on the narrow hardpacked snow, I paused when hearing Tom utter a low "Uhhh!" followed by a quiet "Aah-ho!" Turning, I watched him take only two or three steps off the trail, then stoop down. He quickly stood up holding a length of snare wire still fastened to a short hardwood stick. A large snowshoe rabbit hung from the wire, the noose tightening around its neck. I had not noticed the rabbit trail that crossed our larger one, nor had I noticed the still live rabbit crouched beside the small maple tree. A single muffled shriek, barely audible, was made by the rabbit as Tom pushed the stick under his jacket belt, leaving the strangling animal hanging at his hip.

All this happened in seconds. I recall being fascinated with the catch, expecting to talk about it. But when Tom immediately stepped back up to the sled's pushing handle, I turned back to the trail and continued pulling. Nothing more was ever said, to me at least, of the rabbit. In another twenty minutes we were at the trail head. As I placed my backpack into the back of

Tom's truck, he quietly undid the snare wire and stick from his belt and gently laid the rabbit beside it. Together we loaded the plastic jugs of syrup. I stashed the sled back along the trail, just off the roadway, while Tom started the truck's engine. Each year my leaving the sugarbush is troublesome to me. Usually quiet, I walk out along the trail, step into the vehicle parked on the reservation dirt road, and with little talk, either drive, or sit while someone else drives, the seven heavily wooded miles back to the village. It's a coming out, a quiet rite of passage. That morning of the rabbit it was no different. My two weeks of near solitude were over. I was forced to anticipate what came next. I appreciated Tom's silence as he turned the truck around and put it through its gears.

During the drive back to the village we talked about how the forest floor was opening up in places of southern exposure. Our anticipation of another spring was evident. Arriving at the village and upon turning into my mother-in-law's yard, I asked how Tom would spend the rest of the morning, what it had in store for him. I don't recall his answer, if there even was one, but I do remember hurriedly taking my pack, bedroll, and snowshoes from the truck and placing them into the house's back shed. After greeting the people in the house—to tell them I was out of the woods—I went back out, grabbing the snowshoes. I tossed them back into the truck, then stepped up into the cab. He said I must plan on doing some walking. After years of knowing Tom I said, simply, "Maybe."

So we drove off again, this time taking a different reservation road. We were going to check Tom's trap line.

I knew about the First Nation people of Canada and their trap lines. Often done by women, Canadian Ojibwe trapping could involve long treks into the bush. In the extreme cases the trapper sometimes camped overnight, alone, miles from home. Everyone on the reserve knew Tom was a trapper.

Tom's line was not that serious. And it wasn't linear, not really a line. Instead, his traps were placed in numerous strategic locations throughout the reservation. He had his own places, carefully chosen to be distant from those of other reservation trappers.

Reservation trapping, like the use of all its resources was monitored by tribal rules and codes. The tribe was no longer completely under the control of local, state and federal—non-tribal authorities. The long-time official oppression had been lifted, somewhat, through recent court decisions regarding sovereignty. So today's reservation people now enjoyed the freedom and responsibility to make and abide by their own laws. But the legacy of a few hundred years of forced change, of oppression, was still troublesome.

The majority culture's certainty that the old foraging adaptation had to give way, that hunting and gathering as a way of life was obsolete and meant to be superseded by something called "civilization," the Ojibwe had to find other ways of surviving. Wage labor came. All this caused some tribal lands to finally fall be owned by outsiders. These parcels, scattered throughout the reservation's boundaries, mean that old patterns of land and shoreline use were difficult to maintain. "No Trespassing" signs and locked gates across centuries-old trails are legion in reservation members' conversations.

So a trap line at Red Cliff today is more of a mosaic, a patchwork quilt of trap settings. While some trappers have accommodated to the impositions of boundary lines, others still attempt to use what they feel is theirs. Lately, there is talk of "getting" the land back, of somehow reclaiming the hunting, fishing and gathering grounds.

Others still attempt to maintain usufructuary rights. They pay little heed to platbook boundary lines, choosing instead to continue to use what they feel is theirs. The people of Red Cliff are typically quiet about this imposition of private ownership, but their frustration sometimes surfaces in outbursts of anger. Well over a hundred years old, the frustration does not go away. Locked gates have been cut down, barriers to entering certain lands pushed aside. And summer and weekend people know that isolated cabins could "spontaneously" combust, to be reduced to ashes.

Tom worked within this larger, difficult context. Tom was known as a serious trapper, a successful one. That season he had taken two fishers, five beavers and several mink. He was especially pleased with the fisher pelts. Fishers were recently reintroduced into Northern Wisconsin to contain what was felt to be a swelling porcupine population. There was talk of how porcupines fed on the tender tops of aspen trees, stunting and deforming them in ways that were detrimental to their use for pulp. Aspens were a cash item for woodcutters who trucked them down to paper mills. But now the fishers were expanding to the point of being, once again, expendable. A trapping season on these large furbearers had been declared, and Tom was in the thick of it. A good pelt brought him $40.00.

As we moved along Blueberry Road out of the village, I studied the clutter inside the truck's cab. No eagle feather, small dream catcher, or leather *ojiihbik* bag hung from the rearview mirror. No conspicuous tobacco pouch lay at the ready. Tom did not smoke or drink anymore. And for some personal reason he seemed unaffected by the resurgent use of feathers, tobacco and other traditional spiritual objects used in rituals.

The items in the truck were what would be expected of a trapper, of someone who worked a sugarbush, or someone who, to a great extent, still lived off the land. Fishing net floats, odds and ends of rope in numerous colors and sizes, cardboard pieces from grocery items—other debris from daily living that clutters our lives, sat on the dashboard, the seat between us and on the floor.

"Where's your plat book?," I asked, referring to the publication of the county that showed who owned its land. Well worn plat books were found in some reservation trucks, those of hunters, trappers, and others who used the land for subsistence purposes. Felt necessary by some, they marked tribal land and those parcels in the hands of outsiders. Some private land owners, sensitive to notions of private property with its boundaries, did not want Indians on it, hunting and gathering.

"Hah," he grunted. And that was his audible answer.

A newly sharpened double bit ax, its head on the floor and its handle up between us, told of something too valuable to be placed in the open back of the truck. I felt comfortable in the jumble. It told me of ease, of the importance of things other than a clean, a neat truck cab. It told me of possessions, of materialism and its relative absence on the reservation.

Tom stopped at his house to pick up fresh bait in case we found any of the traps disturbed, any that needed resetting. Several years ago he and his sons built a two-storied log house on the north side of the village, just up from Chicago Creek. Since the passing of his wife last year he lived alone in the large structure. I felt that, perhaps, he was a bit lonely, alone in those rooms. Last year in the deep of winter I found him sitting before a television set in the subdued light of an overcast day, wanting it seemed, to talk. He fixed coffee and we spent an hour or so in quiet conversation.

His wife's ashes had recently been placed in a grave behind the house at the edge of the clearing back there. "That's where I'll be someday," he said. "Right there by those aspens, under that big balsam." I told him it looked like a good place to me, as good as any. But that day he was uneasy, commenting on how when alone in a house you hear sounds that otherwise go unregistered. It had been an unusually cold winter, temperatures bottoming out near thirty below Fahrenheit, and the house's roof boards occasionally cracked from the frost.

I read his remarks as concern about spirits, those that were known to come a-calling in the months after a death. They came, it is believed, to take the living along with them on their return to the hereafter. "I never did anything to her," he said. "I treated her good, never hit her."

As is the case with many of the reservation residents, here was a man, then in his late sixties, who was raised with the severe strictures of the Catholic Church—as well as the old Ojibwe teachings—and who somehow lived in both of these worlds.

Living in two worlds can be invigorating, even fulfilling in a myriad of rich ways, but it can also carry a price. Sometimes its burden can be overwhelming, even defeating. Those successful at it must be masters of change, of adaptability—and of strength.

Sitting in the truck while he went into the house for the bait, I surveyed his yard. At first, perhaps, it might have seemed to be in a state of some disarray, a conclusion I would have drawn when first coming to the reservation nearly forty years ago. But that morning I knew differently. It was the yard of a hunter, a trapper, a man who in all seasons set nets in the big lake, and who knew where the forest's plants, the roots, leaves, flowers and bark could be readily found. It was a yard filled with the tools he used in his life.

In a scene similar to the one I found myself in that sunlit March morning, Canadian writer Hugh Brody, in his important little book entitled *Maps and Dreams,* concludes that such a yard was normal, adapted to the lives of those who lived in the yard's house. People who live off the land go to it in all seasons, using it, interacting with it. The tools they need to survive, those not immediately in use, should be near at hand, at the ready. To Brody, such an apparent "messy yard" was not messy at all. It was a beautiful statement about how the "owners" lived, how they met life's changing demands, how they were at peace with their world.

Hugh Brody noted how some of Canada's First Nation people live off their lands by going to different resource locations in different seasons. This way, they have several "yards," each with its own house. Thus, what we outsiders call yards might better be seen as *encampments.* As such, the houses are not focal points. Instead, it is the land and the tools needed to harvest its offerings that are primary.

Tom's material possessions — his tools — were handled almost casually. Sometimes I felt there was a measured *distance* between him and them. He did not dwell on them, did not fetishize them.

With Brody's words echoing in my mind, I noted how Tom's

fishnets were drying in the sunlight and renewing air. I saw his
dented aluminum boat upturned, lasting-out the winter.
Sugarbush items—three-pound metal coffee cans, five gallon
white plastic pails, and others were being collected and would,
one day, be hauled out to camp to replace those now in use
when the time came. I saw piles of firewood and a large splitting area with its comfortable, soft blanket of chips and bits of
bark, all telling of the good labor that the task of splitting firewood offers. A *jitamo*, the little red squirrel, sat upon the chop-
ping block, enjoying the oily seeds buried deep in a pine cone.
A line stretched between two trees held the head and a skinned
shank of a white tailed deer, recently taken for food. The yard
was as it should be.

In a recent study of King Philip's War, fought in New England in 1675 and 1676, historian Jill Lepore suggests that three
hundred years ago the colonists' houses were obvious cultural
markers that set the English apart from the tribesmen. The
English, to a great degree, based much of their personal identity
upon their houses. To them "the Savages'" wigwams were not
worthy of the label: "house." The Wampanoags, Narragansetts,
Nimucks, and Pocumtucks knew this. In the war, they set out
to destroy these English structures, to reduce them to ash. They
knew such acts struck at the very core of colonial identity. The
tribesmen also worked to pull down the Englishmen's fences,
these symbols of foreign "ownership."

Like Tom, the Wampanoags and other tribal nations felt at
home in a much wider world than that bounded by the walls of
a house, the fence of a yard or a field. Their "fields" were much
larger. And over three hundred years later, Tom's "fields" were
these Red Cliff woods and the big lake. Somehow, in my pon-
dering of all this, three hundred years and New England did
not seem so distant.

Back in the truck and on the road again, we headed out to
Frog Bay. Tom's family was known to have set nets at Frog Bay
beach and to set traps back along the slough that reached a half-
mile or so into the woods. He parked the truck at the trail head

of the mile-long path leading down to the slough. Luckily, I felt, the snow was not deep. I left the snowshoes in the truck. We moved along the trail without speaking. Following behind him, I studied this man, his movements, his observations in the woods. His stocky figure, feet clad in rubber soled snow-packs, with a pair of grey thick wool pants, a quilted tan winter jacket, and a woolen cap, a toque, pulled over his ears, fit in well among those trees. This was very familiar territory to him for he, his many siblings, their parents and grandparents had all used Frog Bay, its creek and slough, and surrounding woods for fishing, hunting and gathering for years and years.

There were no settings along the trail, only two at the water's edge, along the creek. We found them, both Number 2's, with jaws still open, the frozen chunks of whitefish still wired to the trap's paddles. They were set between the spreading roots of two large spruce trees. Large pieces of white plastic PVC piping, about a foot and a half in length, were wired in place before each.

"Why the PVC?" I asked.

Tom, in his usual way, did not answer as he used a foot to brush snow away from the tree roots. Then he said, "It looks funny, doesn't it? Way out here in the woods. Catches your eye."

"Sure does," I replied. "It should be down in somebody's basement, carrying their waste water away."

After another delay Tom finally got right to the answer. "That mink is curious—what's the word? — inquisitive? He sees it too, and he comes to investigate. He likes to crawl into small openings. He'll want that whitefish."

That was about the extent of our talking on that hike to Frog Creek. Only one other incident brought words. While heading back out, after a few hundred yards, when I stopped to watch and listen to the woods, when he was several yards ahead of me I said to him, "This is where I would like to come some day and sit, all day, to see what goes on out here." He paused and turned to see what I was referring to. I pointed to a stump beside the trail. His reply was simply "You'd get cold enough."

Back at the truck we climbed in and headed north, down Frog Bay Road. Nearing its end, Tom slowed down, then stopped, as he craned his neck to see into the woods beside the road. "Nope," not today, he concluded as he drove on. It was another trap setting, this time at the mouth of a metal culvert that lay hidden under the roadway. "That's a good place for fishers," he said. "They use culverts to cross the road, stay out of sight."

Then it was a drive out along Blueberry Road. Another trap was set beside the road, at the foot of a large oak tree. For this one we had to leave the truck and step into the woods. The bait was gone. Instead of a section of a large PVC pipe, this setting had two short pieces of aluminum flashing tacked to the tree and flanging outward into a large "V" in which the trap sat.

"Acorns," I was told. "They get hungry in late winter. Acorns can carry them until the snow leaves."

"What are you after here?," I asked.

"Fisher mostly, but really anything that comes along," he replied.

This is the way it went. We drove the reservation roads, stopping now and then, sometimes not leaving the truck, but always checking traps. There were eighteen of them, except for those at Frog Creek, all set along the roadway.

On the way back to my mother-in-law's house, Tom started to chuckle. "You didn't have to use your snowshoes, did you? What did you think—we'd be gone for a few days—half way to Corny?" Corny is a reference to Cornucopia, a town west of the reservation. Our trip, our ride, took about an hour and a half. If it weren't for the walk into Frog Creek it would have been under an hour.

"Your're a modern trapper," I said, reaching for my door's handle, as we pulled into my in-law's yard.

"Hey," Tom countered. "It's too bad you won't be here Monday. You could come along when I drive out to Sand River to check my beaver traps. That's a good two hour trip."

At Red Cliff, technology has brought change while it, in a sometimes confusing irony, helps maintain tradition.

Tom had not spent his entire life on the reserve. He served years of military time in the Pacific during World War II. One morning at breakfast in the sugarbush cabin he started telling me the story: his being trained to establish a beachhead on islands held by the Japanese; his mountain fighting on the islands of the Philippines; his killing the enemy and carrying a dead white officer on his shoulder off the mountain; his using the Ojibwe language with a colleague to get radio messages through for proper artillery use; and finally, after the cessation of hostilities, his involvement with prisoner exchanges in Korea.

After many unsuccessful tries to get him to tell me this story, it all came out, unexpectedly one morning. He talked so long that I ran out of tapes.

In his younger days, Tom was a good baseball player. Stories are told of games he pitched for the Red Cliff teams of the 1940's and 1950's. I recall the day in the early 1960's when he was pressed into play for the Bayfield team in a game against Lac du Flambeau. His fastball was just as I had been told it was. The men from Flambeau did not catch up to it.

And he played baseball in other places. Right after the war he and his wife moved to New Jersey. Here, too, Tom pitched, and played, undefeated for a sandlot team. His brother-in-law, a native of New Jersey, loved to tell me the story.

But most of this was of a time before I began coming to Red Cliff. Except for the morning in the sugarbush and the World War II story, I was not able to get him to share these early times with me. While he was known for his loud boasting when drinking—his drinking and smoking had stopped the last two decades I knew him—to me he was always quieter, always at peace. Perhaps by my time he had decided to settle in, to live out his time on the reservation.

In 1969 he was a role player in a federal court case that ended over one hundred years of unjust federal and state control over hunting and fishing for Ojibwe people. Yet in much of the literature on this case his name is not included. The media focused on the raising of a fish net in Lake Superior (and on an incident of deer hunting in the St. Croix Ojibwe community). The six Red Cliff men who raised the net that morning in 1969 were arrested and released on bail. They were later found not guilty. But it was Tom, along with another reservation man, who set the net in the darkness of the night before. This quiet, behind the scenes political action was, to me, typical of Tom. In the dark of night he rowed out onto Gichigami and set a fish-net, something he had done most of his life. And like his military experiences, he did not boast about this.

This image of a man who was in the depths of battle in the war in the Pacific in the 1940's, and who returned to the reservation to partake in another battle is at the heart of my memories of Tom. In his hunting, trapping, fishing and gathering at Red Cliff, he quietly went about his business. He was at home on the big lake and in the woods of the reservation shoreline.

The Progressive Dinner

A capital bean soup with fresh venison,
steamed in the centre, with berries and
other sweets--
— Johann Georg Kohl, among
the Ojibwe in 1855

In the early 1970's, a rage was the progressive dinner. Like Friendship Bread (a simple homemade twist of bread meant to be made and given along with a copy of its written recipe, to a neighbor—an act that was to domino through a neighborhood) the notion was to build community. Not quite the same as the "I'm O.K.—You're O.K." years, those of the progressive dinner were at least of a closely related genre. Perhaps in those times the country was aware of an ominous distancing occurring between us. Maybe we were trying to get to know each other again.

Such a dinner was the reason for a family event at Red Cliff almost thirty years ago. It stands as an example of cultures trying to accommodate each other, attempting to work things out, but in the end not succeeding. Still, the attempt was made, a good time was had, another family gathering was orchestrated and carried out. There was laughter, good food, and perhaps even some violin music in the background.

The women planned it. My wife, Marlene, and I were to drive up to Red Cliff on Friday evening after work. That would ensure she had ample time to help her mother prepare her dinner entree. The meal was to be Saturday evening.

In case you have forgotten, a progressive dinner starts at one house and moves, progresses, on to others, one entree at a time. It was all the rage for the city folk for a few years. At Red Cliff we talk of "Feedings," and of "Feasts." Rarely is the more formal word "dinner" used. There is an elderly feeding site and more and more community feasts are held. "Dinner" is a word from outside, perhaps with pretention. So once again, the name of something, the word used to describe something, becomes a matter to ponder.

The act of cooking at Red Cliff involves more than preparing food. And it is more than merely another aspect of a community's division of labor. In my experience most reservation cooking is done by women, but some men are known for their skill as cooks. Perhaps this is nothing more than the custom in the Western World wherein most of the everyday domestic work of the kitchen is done by the woman, while food preparation done in the finest hotels and eateries is typically done by males. It is as if the ordinary, the necessary and perhaps drudgingly domestic chores are relegated to the female, while the more festive, prestigious cooking was turned over to the chef, who usually is male. These sorts of role reversals are not uncommon throughout the world.

Red Cliff cooking done by males might also be related to the economic system of the reservation that has emerged in the past few decades. Since World War II, reservation unemployment levels have seen peaks and valleys. Job training has been a program oftimes pushed by the Bureau of Indian Affairs. In this context, reservation men have sometimes enrolled in various technical courses and been employed as cooks. Area restaurants sometimes have a Red Cliff man doing much of their cooking. While some ethnologists indicate that Ojibwe women did most of the cooking, it is also clear that at times, such as told by John Tanner in the early 1800's (see *A Narrative of His Captivity* and *Adventures of John Tanner*), when a man could be out in the winter woods, alone for days and even weeks at a time, that he became the food preparer.

So there are households in Red Cliff in which the man, at times, will prepare a meal. This is not at all unusual. The verb "to cook" is used carefully at Red Cliff. When a woman announces she is going to cook today, she is saying she will prepare a, perhaps, large meal for more than the usual people who daily come to her table. An announcement that someone is going to cook is an invitation for others to come to eat. It is also, I suggest, a statement that someone has something to cook, that the larder is full. Traditionally, in a hunting society, the kill was shared by an extended family, or even the entire community. Such sharing was reciprocal, expected to be done when others had full larders. It was insurance of a sort, a hedge against times when the hunter came home empty handed. It worked to ensure the survival of the community.

I'm not sure when the fad of progressive dinners died out. Maybe a few retrograde thinkers still hold them, but progressive dinners have dropped out of the media chatter. I cannot recall when I last noticed people still doing them.

The ideal progressive dinner built upon itself and was to accumulate in the stomach slowly, a little at a time. A truly social affair, it was a time to enjoy good food and conversation over an extended period of time, and importantly, in several different settings. A consummate example of a custom come to fruition in an accumulative society, it allowed participants to enjoy each other's company over dinner, but just as importantly, to show off their houses, their creativity in material use, their economic success.

So when a progressive dinner is held it is expected the houses or apartments, condos, town-homes or whatever are involved will be "looked over," put on display, asking for commentary. This is in stark contrast to an Ojibwe custom. The old texts tell where a person comes to a lodge, is asked in, takes a seat by the fire and remains silent for an hour or much more. Surely such a guest took stock of the lodge, but he or she was not expected to comment on it. Progressive dinners are meant to be chatty affairs, abuzz with excited talk of foods, household items and other domestic subjects.

Sociologists speak of a conspicuous consumption found in stratified societies. That's us. We consume conspicuously and we certainly are stratified. The two are longtime bedfellows. Our consumption is another way to announce who we are. But on the reservation it can be different. At Red Cliff there is a reticence to speak at length about material possessions. Rather, a careful attempt is made not to focus on them, to gush over them, to announce their possession.

This obvious non-materialism is always a strong undercurrent in personal relationships. One does not fawn over a new car, or a new kitchen floor. A freshly painted kitchen is, perhaps, remarked upon, but then the conversation moves on. Here on The Rez, material things do not usually demand explicit consideration. Such a detailed enquiry could be considered inappropriate, perhaps even "going too far," something that might be considered too personal.

The old tale of the person who complimented the Indian upon the beauty of his new shirt, only to have the Indian peal it off and hand it to him has some truth to it. Things are shared on the reservation, certainly between family members and outward in larger concentric circles. Several times over the past forty years I was quietly embarrassed to have been given a personal or household item after I commented upon it, apparently going to extremes in adoration of it.

Tribal communities come in many types and forms, some more stratified than others, but in all the ethic of sharing is expressed in ways greater than in contemporary United States and Canadian society. And pressures to share are found at Red Cliff. Not only internally, they are also found between reservations.

Recently, a case of revenue sharing on the part of the Wisconsin Potawatomi Nation showed how these pressures to sahre are extant between tribes. The fact that the Ojibwe and Potawatomi were once united into a larger, earlier tribe, that they both speak an Algonkian language is important in this. The Potowatomis' willingness to share their casino generated revenues with Red Cliff might be viewed as unusual to some, but to The People it is seen in a different way.

Sharing is certainly the essence of a progressive dinner. Food is shared between households, in some cases between friends or relatives. The dinner I write of was between extended family members. And, right from the start the event had a ring of humor to it. Most participants chuckled with its idea, knew such dinners were popular in cities and were written about in newspapers. A progressive dinner on the Rez? The idea brought smiles.

A sister-in-law, a *summa cum laude* at a Midwestern university in Social Work who married into the tribe, was at the heart of the affair. Always a treasure, she is innovative, clever, and planning one event after another—most designed to enhance the closeness of the extended family. I look upon our progressive dinner as one of her masterpieces.

The extended family is just that. At that time, nearly twenty-five years ago, it extended outward to include three sets of uncles and aunts, five sets of married siblings, one grandmother (all other grandparents were gone by the 1970's), and twelve grandchildren. That makes twenty-seven people. Today the family measures into the forties.

The dinner was to serve as a New Year's celebration, held in late January, when the activities of Christmas have passed. It started with a cup of soup at an elderly aunt and uncle's small house. This couple was prominent in the family. It was considered affluent, having benefitted from years of employment in "sailing." ("Sailing" referred to hiring on as a worker on the numerous iron ore carriers that moved ore from Duluth and Silver Bay in Minnesota to down-lakes ports like Cleveland, Ohio, and Gary, Indiana.)

Imagine upwards of thirty people—youngsters included—converging on a small three-room house for a cup of soup. That scene in itself was humorous, but the organizers were certain it could all be handled quickly and that the group—now with the soup-serving aunt and uncle included with the throng—would move on to the second home.

Sometimes the best laid plans do go awry. Upon entering this first house I noted, again, its warmth and coziness. I always felt welcome in those small rooms. This evening, we were all busy finding our sitting or standing places when the soup was served. No cups of soup here. We were served bowls, large bowls of an old reservation favorite: hominy soup.

The hominy had been secured from a friend on the Bad River reserve, east of Ashland, about fifty miles away. Some Ojibwe people continue to make hominy, to wash the dry corn kernels in wood ashes (the old way) instead using a can of household lye. It's a time-consuming task, taking a few days. When served a bowl of hominy soup at Red Cliff you know its worth. Often with venison included, a coloring of carrots, the dish is hearty and filling. It is Ojibwe soul food.

But this was a progressive dinner. The soup was meant to be a start to the meal, an appetizer, really. I could not eat only one cup of hominy soup. I suspect few people who understand it can. You must have more. So, moving on into dangerous waters, I accepted a second ladle of the hot potion. And, with the value of "the good eater" on the Rez, it would have been quite impolite not to have more. The uncle and aunt knew the symbolism of food. They understood that houseguests were to be inundated with food, to be encouraged to go back for more.

This, then, was the scene at the first stop of the dinner's progression. For me, and others, it should have been the only stop. Hominy soup needed the accompaniment of bread and butter, thick slices of the aunt's homemade bread. All this needed to be washed down with water, coffee, or milk.

The second stop was at another aunt and uncle's small house, close by, and like the first, overlooking Lake Superior. Here the going was a bit easier. The entree was salad. There is, perhaps, always room for salad. How much stomach space can a few thin leaves of lettuce fill? So we ate bowls of salad. It turned out to be the familiar Iceberg lettuce, shipped in from California. Ours was dressed with a tomato based French dressing, tangy and light orange in color.

Again, we were expected to eat. And somehow we did, but the laughter was beginning to mount, the chiding about taking more. I glanced at my wife and saw she was still holding up, complimenting her aunt on how good her salad tasted, how well it turned out.

Then came the serious entrees—the meat and potatoes of the dinner. We drove our caravan of cars down Blueberry Road to a trailer house, the home of my wife's sister and her husband. Here it was, the roast turkey and mashed potatoes with gravy. The bird was cut, the potatoes scooped, the gravy ladled. We were admonished if we did not take a good portion. One must work at being known as a good eater.

On the downhill ride now, we moved onto the fourth house, this one in the midst of a tribal housing project. It was in a two-family side-by-side structure. Here we were served a vegetable dish, one of the baked sort with cream of mushroom soup as the thickener. Slivers of almonds lying on its crusty top. A good-enough entree, even with the mushroom soup, it was, I thought, a meal in itself. And such a dish cannot stand on its own legs, it needs bread, butter, water, milk. Liquids take up space, create volume. However, especially for those of us from the city, one liquid was conspicuously absent: no wine was poured at this meal.

Then it was to the grandmother's house, the one that was the center of the entire family. Here we were expected to feast on fry bread and a green Jello salad. More bread. More salad. How could anyone not take a piece of hot fry bread? Perhaps the epitome of Indian soul food, it marked out identity. We had to eat.

Finally, lastly, it was the ride into nearby Bayfield, to the house of a brother-in-law and his wife who were to serve dessert and coffee. Dessert was in the form of a few pans of creamy bars with the name of "Better Than Sex." We came, we ate and drank. We all expressed our discomfort.

Today, thirty some years later, our one and only progressive dinner has become a family story. It is told with shrieks of disbelief and with exclamations like, "Thank God we don't do things like that anymore!" and, "I still see the size of those soup bowls!" Just the mention of a progressive dinner brings high-pitched shrieks of laughter.

Meals at Red Cliff are typically eaten in a dignified silence. While a few family members might wolf their portions down, the older members take much time, chewing each bite as if in deep appreciation. In the old tribal ideologies, food is a gift from the *manidoog*. It is never taken without thankfulness. And at Red Cliff the giving of thanks can be a solemn affair, a personal, quiet ritual.

Gift giving was not, and today still is not, a matter of little import. Gifts are mediatory. They move along paths of relationships. They carry obligation. It's all about reciprocity. So a meal, especially something labeled a feast, is a somewhat solemn affair. This can be seen at some of today's pow wows where participants are invited to share in a free meal. The line might be long, but generally a quietness abounds. People tend to eat in silence, accepting, willingly receiving their gift. This is the Ojibwe way.

So the progressive dinner did not involve long thoughtful conversations. The meals I am part of on the reservation never do. Even over dessert and coffee, the standard time for the "lighting of cigars in the drawing room," such talk did not surface. By that time we were overly sated anyway. Relaxing, meaningful talk would have been out of the question.

We see the folly of the progressive dinner today. The laughter it engenders comes from an unstated awareness of its pretension. In those years a few of us were fresh from the city. We thoughtlessly tried to bring some of that to the reservation. And, as demanded by the rules of traditional Ojibwe society, we and our ideas were courteously received. The uncle who had spent a lifetime gorging himself at a table accepted the fact of his being served only a bowl of salad and then being expected to leave the house, to go on for the next course. He made accommodations. Respectfully, he accepted the new ways, at least for the evening.

We see how the extended family took this new custom and, although it was given only one chance, it was changed to suit the family's notions of proper behavior. Heaping portions of food were served to each comer, and each was exhorted to "eat lots." Then at the next house the scene unfolded again. The solid, old norm of sharing was honored, kept alive. As the family tried, then rejected, the progressive dinner, we were moved further along the path of self-acceptance. We knew who we were and who we were not. Most importantly, we recognized a conciliation flowing through us.

But this communal sharing of resources does more than fill each person's needs. It ripples outward to the larger world. In a community where the ethic of accumulation is not trumpeted, and in fact is negatively sanctioned, the effect on the resources is noticeably less. Today a hunter may knock down a deer, then give portions of it to several households. A good catch of lake trout also can make the rounds. A person's wild rice and maple syrup also usually shows up on many different tables. Finally, the old cliche about "the Indian" using natural resources is true: What is taken from the land is used in its entirety. In such a community, less really is more. Under these conditions, and with proper controls on human population growth, natural resources could be perpetually maintained, allowed to renew. Approached traditionally, wild rice beds are not overharvested. The deer herd is not wiped out with a single season's harvest. In such a setting, humans walk lightly on the land.

A Need for Paint

When I was first came to the reservation in 1959, I found a cluster of grey, weathered wood frame houses settled onto the earth throughout the shoreline woods. Some sat in or near open places that at one time must have felt the cut of the steel moldboard plow. These old fields were being reclaimed, as aspens, white and yellow birches, white pines, spruces, hemlocks, and balsams worked to take root at their collapsing borders. These clearings were the old reservation farms of a hundred years earlier.

A few houses were on the small lots of the Buffalo Subdivision at Buffalo Bay. Most of the rest were stretched out along the unnamed dirt road heading north to Frog and Raspberry Bays. Some were further out, up on what was jokingly called "Pagan Hill."

In 1960, there were approximately twenty-five such houses on The Rez. This was before the coming of "housing projects" and the mobile homes that now are almost ubiquitous at Red Cliff.

Weathered, unpainted houses. Typically small, but most with a second story, they suggested a time of some affluence, or a time of an abundance of newly sawn pine lumber. These structures had replaced the earlier, homemade low log houses of the late 1800's. With few exceptions, they had replaced what were derogatorily called tar paper shacks. (Now slipping out of the country's lexicon, tar paper is being replaced with the term "roofing felt.") The relatively inexpensive heavy tarred paper repelled water, so it was used to cover the exterior walls of wooden structures. Today, no one lives in "tarpaper shacks" at Red Cliff.

One or two of the wood framed houses were called "Sears Roebuck houses," ordered from catalogs. Others were said to be built during "the lumbering days." And all needed paint—or so I thought.

It is said that a coat of paint can do wonders. It freshens things up, hides a multitude of sins. And—there is a rainbow of colors. So in my naivete—in 1963—I started to paint my mother-in-law's house. The new son-in-law took brush in hand.

I recall how at first the weather-hardened clapboards resisted the oily paint. The first strokes of the brush laid on a layer that sat atop the ridges and weathered grooves of the ancient pine. The decades-old resin still did its work: repelling the foreign substance. Beads formed on top of the boards, but with a second and then a third stroke, the paint won out. It spread to the deepest groove, finally soaking in. Grey, weather-hardened clapboards began to disappear. They became a bright, glaring white. But the narrow, small houses had *two* stories and I had no long ladder, only a lightweight wooden stepladder.

After a few hours an uncle appeared. He surveyed the situation and left, returning not only with a long, wooden extension ladder, but more paint, more brushes. Uncle Lionel, a brother of my mother-in-law, regularly appeared to do carpentry and other jobs at the house. It was what uncles did. With no limitations of strength, he was able to maneuver the dark grey—like the old house, it too was weathered—heavy ladder up to the two high roof peaks. His arms did not tire from the rhythmic movement of the brush over the thirsty boards.

Sunday afternoon came and I had to return to the city. My wife and I packed up and drove off. The painting was finished by the uncle. The old reservation house was painted white. What had I started? What had we done? The house was still small and of a very old vintage. It was worn, its back doorless "shed" standing attached to the small kitchen wall, askew, leaning like a tree reaching for sunlight.

The tiny wooden outhouse in the back yard, also painted, matched the house's new brightness. Both stood out like beacons in that grassy, comfortably unkempt yard. Goldenrod, the pleasant softness of wild plum brush, the tall forming heads of wild timothy hay, bordered the clearing. Lake Superior, bright and deep as a blue eye, lay to the east as if studying the house, contemplating its new color. Surely, a new time had arrived.

Two ancient apple trees—both Whitney Crabs—that stood beside the house, were left in their brushy, obviously untended, carefree state. Suddenly their thick, dark green growth contrasted in a harsh way with the house. They were still wild. One of these old trees still stands, glorious in its neglect.

My father-in-law and I would spend hours on summer afternoons lying on the ground beneath it, watching vehicles pass on Highway 13, less than a hundred feet away. Sometimes we shared beer or wine, letting its soothing essences fuzz our words. At such times he would begin a colloquy about the tree, how in spring its fragrant blossoms were sought by bees, how they did their labor of love to use the tree's nectar for their honey. He intimated that the old bedraggled tree was important to him. Perhaps that is why it still stands.

Where I came from, unpruned apple trees were unheard of. Grey, bare, unpainted clapboards meant carelessness, even poverty. Apple trees needed to be pruned and houses needed paint. Paint preserved the wood. The fact that these particular Red Cliff clapboards, perhaps as much as 120 years old, had done very well without it, never registered with me. They had to be covered, *coated,* with white paint.

Writing on August 21, 1880, Red Cliff's new Indian Agent at the time, S. E. Mahan, like me was enamored with white paint. He wrote, in his first annual report to the Commissioner of Indian Affairs, of his pleasure in working with the native people in his entire La Pointe agency (at the time it held seven different reservations):

"The Indians are very quiet and orderly; not so much dancing or counselling and more work. The axe, grub-hoe, plow,
seed, and the scythe receive more of their time; thus, we see
them lay off and forsake one by one those old customs and heathenish habits, by adopting those of civilization."

Agent Mahan continued his praise, this time speaking spe-
cifically about the people at Red Cliff:

"There is gradually developing itself a feeling of emulation
among them. Antoni Buffalo, chief, set a good example to his
people this summer by painting his house white; he is worthy of
mention, energetic, shrewd, and a hard worker, and is succeeding well in his endeavors."

The Buffalo family has a long history of leadership at Red
Cliff. The label, *shrewd,* used by Agent Mahan to characterize
Antoine in 1880, fits the description of this man given me by
one of his elderly descendants at Red Cliff in a long series of
interviews I had with him in the 1970's and 1980's. In these
interviews, John Buffalo, born in 1905 at Red Cliff, told me
how enterprising his ancestor Antoine was, how he ran his large
general store and handled his numerous land parcels.

My tattered dictionary defines emulation this way: "Ambi-
tion or endeavor to equal or excel; rivalry." Apparently there
can be more to white paint than simply preserving raw, uncov-
ered pine clapboards. In 1880, Agent Mahan was joyful in seeing the new white house at Red Cliff. It seemed clear that this
was the first painted house on the reserve, and that he hoped
that other community members would follow their leader's example. Perhaps it is good that he was not around some eighty
years later to witness the plethora of grey, unpainted houses on
his old reserve, but he would doubtlessly have been pleased when
I naively spread on that first stroke of thick white exterior enamel
in 1963.

Our worlds are constructed in the process of our growth.
My world held images of painted farm houses, of a grandmother—born in 1876, the year of Custer's demise—who kept

a shelf of old paint cans, brushes and a gallon of turpentine at the ready. Each spring she seemed to be painting something, making it anew. Born into an immigrant farm household in the sandy bottoms of south-central Wisconsin, near the community then called Grand Rapids (she said its name was later changed to Wisconsin Rapids, because of confusion with the Michigan city with the same name) she knew a life of work, the value of the dollar. Frugal, as the descendents of German peasants had to be in the America of that time, she had witnessed the changes wrought by the Industrial Revolution. Born into a horse culture, she saw the upheaval of the coming of the automobile.

This is the woman who dug the wild horseradish roots that grew in the roadside ditch of Highway 38 beside our farm in the 1940's in southern Wisconsin. I have images of her standing at a homemade bench behind the farmhouse, while streams of semi-trucks passed loudly on their commercial routes out on the highway. Eyes watery, tearful, she grated the roots outside, hoping a breeze lessened the sting of the rising perfume. She made lye soap from the pig fat left at the annual fall butchering on the farm. (She was a teetotaler, but on butchering day she would down a shot of brandy.)

This is the grandmother who was still in the clutches of the Victorian Age, as much as someone in the working class, the rural "farming class" of America, could be. She revered white skin. When obligated to be outdoors for extended periods of time, as when she worked in her kitchen vegetable and flower garden, she wore a cloth bonnet, of her own making, with wooden slats sewn into the flange that kept the sun from her face. And she hoed her rows of vegetables with arms and hands covered with an old pair of cotton stockings—holes cut for her fingers.

She knew the value of a coat of paint.

This wonderful grandmother, still alive in my memory, still important in how I see myself, must have been behind me that Saturday of the Red Cliff house painting.

Urban paintathons interest me. They are culturally specific, fitting into a particular time and place. They seem to be for the benefit of the house owner, usually a community member suffering some hardship, as well as for those doing the painting. Paintathons as an example of volunteerism are ubiquitous in America. They tell us something of our values, of who we are.

I was reminded how we register the impact of coming upon an old, unpainted house several years ago when a president appointed a judge from New Hampshire to the nation's Supreme Court. At that time Justice Seuter lived in a wonderfully unpainted wood frame house (with his mother, I think), a house that seemed to fit well into the mountainous landscape of New England.

We television viewers were shown the outside of the house, then taken inside. It was filled with books—at least my memory tells me it was. I was taken by the beauty of the contrast. Here was a man, although said to be a conservative, that went to my heart. I loved his unpainted house, his life of the intellect. Maybe I loved him. And with afterthought, the early perceived juxtaposition of an old, grey, weathered house, with someone in the judiciary is wonderful. There is more to life than painted houses.

There was one more time I was involved in a "house painting" on the reservation. It, too, commands reflection. A large community hall stood facing the highway at Buffalo Bay, in the center of what was the "village" in the 1960's. In fact, this is the building in which the community meal was served the afternoon my wife and I were married in the nearby Catholic church. Interestingly, the building turned its back upon Lake Superior, choosing instead to face the highway. Perhaps that is because it was built in the 1930's as a Works Progress Administration project. In those years, it seems, tribal leaders were more oriented to the mainstream, having to deal with the reality of governmental programs that, at base, were still meant to assimilate the Indian into United States society.

As I understand it, someone, a "white man" living distant

from the reservation was troubled by the grey, weathered structure. He offered to donate paint for its "improvement." All the details have escaped me, but I recall the weekend set aside for the work. At that time the word "paintathon" had apparently, not yet been coined. Again, my wife and I drove up to be part of it, to help out.

Only a dozen or so tribal members showed up. In true community fashion it was a social affair, filled with laughter, teasing, and a festive air. There were sandwiches, a large kettle of homemade vegetable soup, someone brought pop, and later a case or two of beer appeared. I was surprised to see the paint. It arrived in numerous one-gallon cans, in a myriad of colors. Most cans had been opened, used, the color of their paint shown in dry dripping rings around the tops. Perhaps from a downstate professional house painter, the paint was the leftovers from jobs—the remnants.

This assortment of colors was mixed together in a barrel and, with some experimentation—colors carefully added now and then—it came out a very deep, chocolate brown. This is the color we spread onto the old boards. It is still the color of the hall—since moved, and currently under renovation—as it stands beside the white clapboard church.

To my knowledge this painting-bee was initiated from outside the reservation. Typical of initiatives meant to improve things in those decades, it was something seemingly more important to outside eyes than those within the community. The history of Red Cliff is replete with such well-meant and usually self-serving activities. The logging of old was meant to help the "Natives." The establishment of the Apostle Islands National Lakeshore—originally seeking to take practically all the reservation's shoreline—was couched in the same values. The park would bring "employment" to the Indians, even though it took most of their land. Community change projects, when coming from the outside, are, by their very nature, suspect.

Interestingly, during a recent summer, in the warm month

of July, I was once again part of a painting bee that involved my mother-in-law's house. In the nearly forty year interim since that weekend back in 1963, the old small house had been covered with an inexpensive composition-board siding, and painted a pale blue. The symbolism of white painted houses that was so important to Antoine Buffalo and Agent Mahan back in 1880 had become passé. But last summer, in the year 2000, the fading blue paint was in obvious need of renewal.

My wife instigated a painting bee, rallying her siblings, her lone surviving uncle, and numerous younger members of the extended family. Even two great-grandchildren (a five- and a three-year-old) of my 80-year-old mother-in-law—youngsters who live in distant New Hampshire—were given brushes to help. It was another sociable gathering of the extended family.

The house was painted in a single day. This time it was a deep chocolate brown. No glaring white paint in the year 2000. I saw the warm, earthiness of the deep brown as another symbol. It seemed to fit better, to settle into the setting of the house. Even old Lake Superior, visible only several hundred yards to the east, seemed to feel comfortable with this natural color. And today I look back at the brown we painted the community hall so long ago as an interesting, although unintended, foreshadowing.

Early twentieth century photos and maps of the reservation exist. One such photo shows a large two-storied structure serving as the Catholic church and grammar school. It is painted a bright white. Even in the old black and white photograph, the brightness of the paint is striking. Elders have told me that in the times of World War I some houses were still showing their first bright coat of paint, but that over the years it wore off.

My 1912 tattered and yellowed Department of the Interior map of Red Cliff uses small black squares for symbols of human-made buildings. At the far southeastern corner of the reserve, right at the water's edge, it shows a Red Cliff Day School with a square beside it, presumably the house for the schoolteacher(s). Moving north along the shore we are given a symbol for the church, again with a black square beside it, perhaps representing the rectory. Then at Buffalo Bay we find a symbol for what is called Red Cliff Station (the terminus of the railway that ran from Bayfield right along the lakeshore). Next to it is another for a logging mill. Three or four apparent squares are located around the railway station.

The cemetery beside Chicago Creek comes next, with a small black square on both its north and south sides. Then no square symbols are shown until we come to Red Cliff (Creek) Bay. Here are symbols for two sawmills, a dock, the "Agency," and three other unidentified buildings.

No other symbols for human habitations are given over the entire reservation. The map shows no roadways except for the two railways. One was built along the lakeshore and the other nearby. This second rail bed arcs to the west immediately after entering the reserve. This is the Bayfield Harbor and North Western Rail Road.

I offer these details because the map is puzzling. Where did the reservation people reside if not in the few square black symbols it gives? Where is Swede Town, the street of houses that stood where the Isle Vista Casino now stands? Surely homes were scattered in other reservation areas, yet the map fails to show them. In 1912, several hundred people lived in Red Cliff. We know there were many more houses on the reserve.

Mike Newago, born in 1918, told me there were "lots of houses" standing along the stretch of Frog Bay Road, just before the big ravine that washes to the nearby lake. These formed a small settlement when he was a youth. In his words, "This was called Raspberry Village because that was where you took the trail to Raspberry Bay." He said they were small log and board houses. Mike did not call them tarpaper shacks.

In 1912, were such houses deemed not to meet the criteria of what, in the non-reservation world, acceptably constituted the concept "house"? Were they, perhaps, in their "uncivilized" (and unpainted) appearance, "invisible" to the government's cartographers, and hence not included in the act of drawing the reservation buildings? Was their fate the same as that of the twenty-three Ojibwe members of a hunting camp on Shadridge Creek east of Mille Lacs Lake that were killed in the great Hinckley (Minnesota) fire of 1894? When the fire's official human death count was tallied, these victims were not included.

Over the years my anthropology textbooks showed photos of wooden frame houses of native people in the Canadian Sub-Arctic. The newer houses, sometimes erected with input from the Canadian government, were painted or perhaps covered with a colored aluminum or vinyl siding, but the older ones seemed invariably to be paintless. Their grey wooden clapboards blended in naturally, and quite comfortably, I thought, with their surroundings.

In such northern societies, the center of a person's identity was (and for many today still is) his or her *kin group,* not a house. Buildings may not be good indicators of their owner's income levels. The deeper personal orientations of life for these people seem to point toward *the family and the land.*

Nearly forty years have passed since I began to paint my wife's parents' house. I still see it, and the other reservation houses, standing in their quiet unpainted defiance. Yet, caught in the tension of a precarious balance between the old and the new, all eventually gave way. One or two old, grey, weathered clapboard houses on the reservation can still be found, but they have been empty, uninhabited, for years. The rest are gone, or at least changed, in one form or another. The old houses that still can be found and are used as present-day habitations are covered in a veneer of paint.

Tobacco
on the Water

We go to nature when we want something.
— **Robert Bly, 1990**

"Untie that line and jump in," he said. "I'll see if I can get this thing started." I had already handed him the two lightweight casting rods, our tackle boxes, the red dented gas can and the two ancient god-awful looking faded and oil-stained seat cushions that were to serve as life preservers.

"D'ja wanta troll?," he asked, bending over the outboard at the boat's stern.

"Sure. But I've never done it."

"Nothin' to it—even a Chimoke can troll," he went on, chuckling. *Chi-mookomaan* is the Ojibwe word for white man. It means long knife, a reference to the swords that some early whites brought to Ojibwe Country so long ago. The People must have been impressed with these long, sharp weapons. Perhaps they wondered about their intended use.

I recall how he went on with his talking, all the time bending over the large and old motor at the rear of the boat. He attached the gasoline line to the red can, threw switches and opened valves as he told about how the fishing was getting good again, about how the lamprey problem was letting up. The trout were coming back after years of extremely low catches. He spoke disparagingly about those saltwater eels and the white sport fishermen, about how, in his words, "They damn near finished fishing for us."

I recall that I tried to chide him, that I said he was wrong. It wasn't the eels or the downstate fishermen, instead it was some exotic virus that was taking the fish. I remember that I told him he did not watch enough "Cronkite"—that he was not well informed.

"Virus hell," he grunted as he stood up to glance at me in the boat's bow. Over the years, he had found too many eel-scarred trout and had lifted a net only to find too few fish. Sometimes a slippery eel would still be attached to a fish. However, lately things were improving. More fish were being taken. It was starting to be good again.

Upon turning back to the engine, he quickly snapped the small black plastic-handled ignition switch, and turned the tarnished brass key. A rich, muffled roar suddenly rose behind him at the stern, bubbling the water. A good, even sound, I concluded it told of a trustworthy motor, well-tuned. We were ready to head out onto the big lake for a few hours of fishing.

Uncle Marv is gone now. That summer's late afternoon of fishing in the channel between Buffalo Bay and Basswood Island must have occurred twenty-five or even thirty years ago. The details, of course, the trivia of the trip are gone as well. But I remember the highlights. Uncle Marv had recently returned to the reservation after another of his extended stays in a distant city and he seemed to need such an excursion on the lake. He needed a fix. I was eager to join him.

Before the last few years of his life, when the sickness became too much, our paths occasionally crossed and we would spend a few hours on the big lake or in the Red Cliff woods. Marv loved to "poke around" as I call it, hiking down old trails, searching out early farm fields now grown over with aspens, and fishing the streams that rush to the lake. He knew where the wild leeks could be found, and where the asparagus beds lay in the old abandoned farmyards. And in fall he loved to search out the best of the gnarled and tangled apple trees that grow here and there along the shoreline.

Always, it seemed, he was on the lookout for the odd-shaped branch that could be rendered into some sort of art piece to be sold to the summer tourists. When he was walking through the woods, his eyes moved from the forest floor up to the trees—searching. It's too bad he didn't take up photography because he had the eye for the unusual. Pieces of clean, white birch bark accumulated in his parents' woodshed, waiting for the next of his projects. He regularly walked the long sand beaches looking for that single piece of driftwood that could easily be turned into a dollar or two.

One year he collected several pieces of shelf fungus, the sort found on dying trees. He painted them, or glued on bright silver and gold sparkling bits of plastic material found in small jars in craft shops. Once he presented me with a long piece of cedar to be used as a name plate for my desk. He had carefully shaped it, then painted my name onto one of its three sides before brushing on layers of shellac. For years it sat on my desk, visible to anyone who stepped into my office.

Marv was one of many who grew up at Red Cliff when there were relatively few summer visitors. A family story tells of his being out at Cornucopia one summer Saturday, where he and a companion had just pulled their small outboard into the harbor after setting a net. They were in the camping park, the one with the large wooden sign with the story of the battle between the Mesquawki (Fox) and Ojibwe that occurred at that spot so long ago. A car of tourists pulled up and Marv was asked to have his picture taken—a real Indian standing beside the sign. Marv charged them twenty-five cents for the photo shoot.

This was not an uncommon event in the earlier days at Red Cliff. Such stories used to bring peals of nervous laughter when told, but more recently the laughter is generally absent at such tellings. If it is present I fail to detect its earlier nervous character. Now the laughter has a different meaning. Perhaps today the overt sensitivity to the politics of those encounters precludes laughter. It has been years and years since I have heard of any tourists asking Red Cliff children standing along the roadside to have their picture taken.

Uncle Marv had been around. He knew the streets of Chicago, Milwaukee, and Minneapolis. Before its destruction in an urban renewal project, Chicago's famed Maxwell Street was well known to him. Once, he was employed in a lumberyard on that city's north side, but he really had held many jobs. He would come and go, spending months at home on The Rez, running trap lines and regularly setting and lifting fishnets, only to suddenly disappear for long periods before unexpectedly turning up again. He was one of those men who were in what social workers in the 1960's called "the reservation-urban cycle." People would leave the reserve to come to the city for a job, only to abruptly go back home when family called, or when certain events demanded. Then, after some time, they would come to the city again to find another job and start over.

Today, for some Red Cliff residents this cyclical pattern of movement to and from distant cities might still linger on, but for most those days are over. It was in the 1960's that a new pattern emerged: the permanent migration of people back home. With this return, now almost fifty years old, many Red Cliff people decided to stay, never to leave again. They were through with the city. In the 1960's, with the advent of community development programs funded by the federal government, jobs became available, pulling people home. Today, for some reserves this return is again peaking due to the jobs reservation casinos are offering.

For the past century such large scale rhythms and cycles— such "circlings"— were a common adaptation at places like Red Cliff. The People had to move here, then there. This was part of mere survival. It was akin to the age-old movement with the seasons that was at the heart of the Ojibwes' earlier subsistence practices. This was how hunters and gatherers lived. Given this as a context, Uncle Marv had adapted well. He knew how, when, and where to move. In this sense he was like the fabled *Wenebozo* who was, it seems, always on the move, traveling from here to there. Like this Ojibwe trickster, Uncle Marv was active, traveling and getting into things. He observed his world—was always on the lookout. *Wenebozo* and Uncle Marv had much in common.

This is the way I remember him on that day on the lake. He observed the water, kept an eye on the sky, and regularly scanned the distant islands, and once out of the marina, he studied the mainland. But that day he also had an air of calmness about him. It seemed to me he had come to the lake to relax and be renewed more so than to catch fish. He wasn't on the lookout for the unexpected or unusual. Perhaps, as I concluded, he had been away too long this time and it was time to get back to what was really important.

Twenty-five or so years ago Uncle Marv would have been in his late forties or early fifties. I was still young—in my early thirties—and we seemed to enjoy our "Uncle-Nephew" relationship. He liked to assume the role of mentor, taking time to teach me things. Yet he also tactfully deferred to my profession as an anthropologist. Like others at Red Cliff, he liked to call me "Professor."

He was starting to show the distended stomach of middle age that some of us wear, and his face was, as usual, quietly flushed. His drinking was still going on and the toll it was taking was quite evident, but through all this he was still displaying a deep degree of intelligence, wit and *joie de vivre*. He was neither short nor tall, and he carried himself with confidence. I had always felt that when at his best he was obviously handsome and neat in appearance. He also was obviously a Native American. He looked like one. His straight, jet black hair, his dark, ruddy complexion, and the shape of his nose and hands all told of it.

That afternoon on the lake we both wore our casual, or "working" clothes. My faded blue jeans were crumpled, my sweat shirt—advertising the University of Minnesota—was old and torn in the right places. My baseball cap was also from "The U" and properly shaped and faded. Marv wore an old pair of green twill work pants and a faded blue and green flannel shirt. His faded baseball cap carried the logo of the Chicago Cubs.

Our boat that day was borrowed from a cousin. Its name, Wet Dream, was painted in black on each side of the bow. The boat was old and well used. It was an 18-foot shell that had been rescued from a weedy corner in someone's back yard in Duluth, and at first glance suggested it was homemade—probably the product of several weekends of labor by an amateur tinsmith who borrowed an acetylene torch or one of those small electric workshop arc welders. Its hull's frame was made from angle iron with several steel panels welded over it. It had been painted a dark green that extended about a foot above the waterline. Above that it was a bright, shiny orange. When I first saw the boat I remember thinking of plastic Halloween pumpkins with their green stems.

The boat's inside was unfinished, having the brown and grey colors of rust, dirt, and a smattering of whitefish scales. The bilge was covered with several loose pieces of plywood carelessly cut to fit, showing the stains of oil, the rounded edges from years of wear and from being left exposed to the elements. There were no seats—only an upturned wooden net box so low that when sitting on it just our heads protruded above the boat's gunwale.

Marv had borrowed the Wet Dream for the afternoon. It was a working Lake Superior fishing boat used to set and raise the long nylon gill nets that caught lake trout and whitefish. It had that authentic commercial fishing boat odor, a mixture of gasoline and fish smells.

I recall how we backed out of the slip and moved easily past the marina's many large sailboats, their lines, in the wind, playing musical notes on the tall and shiny metal masts. The sail-boats' brightly painted hulls lay proudly beneath chrome-studded gleaming topsides. These were the pleasure boats of the downstate Wisconsin and Twin Cities people. These were the people who, twenty or so years ago, had started to come to the lake in increasing numbers. In the more immediate post-World War II years, few such sailboats were seen on the lake. But now the word was out. The Apostle Islands and the Red Cliff shoreline—along with nearby Bayfield and Cornucopia—were becoming playgrounds for the affluent.

Turning the corner of the breakwall, we headed out into Buffalo Bay and into the two-mile wide channel between Basswood Island and the mainland. Uncle Marv, standing back in the stern, increased speed, and the boat, its bow rising a bit, settled its stern down onto and into the lake. It seemed to be at home, comfortable with the cold water as it cruised smoothly ahead. I remember being surprised at how well it moved, how seaworthy it appeared to be.

Even though we had each brought a small tackle box, our gear was minimal. I found a large red and white spoon, snapped it to my leader and cast it out behind the boat. Handing Marv his rod and reel, I recall taking the motor's handle while he baited his line. I recall that he mentioned how lucky a certain blue and white spoon had been for him in spring when he last was on the water. Once both rods were ready Marv stuck them into the brackets mounted at the boat's stern.

"This is trolling," he said. "Easy, huh?" Then, taking the throttle again, he pointed the bow south. The plan was to troll down to Roy's Point and coast back in the strong wind coming up the channel. We agreed it would save gasoline.

After relinquishing the throttle to him, I stood beside him at the stern and watched our lines play out behind the boat, one on each side of the wake. Marv reached to his shirt pocket and pulled out a package of Old Gold cigarettes. He offered the pack to me and I took one. Then he tapped one out, took it with his puckered lips, put the pack back and soon produced a lighter and lit up.

He knew I no longer smoked and all the while looked quizzically at me, apparently wondering whether I would light up or not. He watched as I leaned over the back of the boat a little and tore the cigarette open and quickly released the tobacco. It fell to the water where it lay, floating as we moved away.

When I straightened up and turned back to Marv, I recall that he muttered something over the quiet hum of the motor. It was something about a "God damned wannabe." Sometimes Uncle Marv accused me of "wanting to be" an Indian.

To the believer, there are spirits in the lake. Perhaps to some, the lake itself is a big, powerful spirit. Then there is the matter of *nibi,* that some say is a spirit in its own right. Yes, sometimes in certain Ojibwe ceremonies, *water* is celebrated in a sacred manner. And as for humans, any time there are spirits, there are responsibilities.

The Jesuit Relations include writings of a Catholic priest, Claude Allouez, from his time in Chequamegon Bay. He was in the bay in 1659 and for a few years following. Among other things, Allouez told how he saw Ojibwe people give things to Lake Superior, because in the words of Allouez, "they felt the lake was a spirit." Back in the mid-1600's this Frenchman probably travelled, now and then, in a canoe in the channel between Basswood Island and Red Cliff precisely where Uncle Marv and I fished. Somehow I find that interesting. Maybe that is part of the reason I made the tobacco offering that day. Maybe I wanted to show that such offerings are still being made.

I do not recall Uncle Marv making any tobacco offerings. If he did these sorts of things he did them out of my presence. Today I wish I had paid more attention when I was with him. I wish I had been able to be more observant, had known what questions to ask. I wish I had not been so young.

Once our lines were baited and out in the water I stood back, leaning on the gunwale, and just watched the lake. When we were well out in the channel I realized that except for a few specks of white off in the distance there were no other boats in sight. I began to be impressed with the obviousness of the water. Its constant, slow motion went nowhere, and like so much of life it travelled not in a straight line from past to present to future, deciding instead, to stay put. It seemed to have collapsed these three places into the here and now. For long moments I remember simply standing there, my forearms on the steel boat, dreamily watching the waves. I recalled my three years in the Navy and how at times I would spend hours seated out on deck just watching the ever-moving ocean.

Then, quietly, as if it sensed it was entering forbidden territory, a white spot appeared around the north end of Basswood. "Here comes the Chippewa," Uncle Marv said. We had both noticed it at the same moment but his greater familiarity with the lake told him instantly it was the large tourist cruise boat from Bayfield. Depending on the vagaries of the wind, we could catch swatches of the tour guide's voice through the ship's amplifier: "...in the main channel again... large pulp rafts from Canada came through here... over 120 feet deep... why the water is so dark... across from Red Cliff now... poor timber on the mainland... logging in the early 1900's..." Then as the boat came closer there was a long pause followed by, "On our port side we're coming up to two fellows trying their luck at trolling."

At that time Marv and I were sitting on the overturned net box, our backs to each other, only our heads visible to the Chippewa's customers. We saw them turn their heads to us almost in unison, like spectators at a tennis match. Then they were past, and the larger boat's wake caught us and we rocked from side to side, gently, as if bowing a few times to the bigger, more powerful craft.

The amplified voice stopped coming to us and as the large boat grew smaller we were left alone again. Nowadays, these approximately twenty-five years later, when I see such a boat with CHIPPEWA loudly painted on its bow and stern I cannot help think of the community meeting I attended several years ago at Lac Courte Orielles—the Ojibwe community about an hour and a half drive south of Red Cliff. A tribal elder, scholar and well-known spiritual leader was standing before the crowd telling us about something when in the course of his presentation he used the phrase, "for those of you who still call yourself CHIPPEWA"—his point being that the label is not what The People really are. It is what the Chimokemaan called them. He meant that The People are Anishinaabe, the word for themselves, in their own language. He meant that CHIPPEWA is a politically loaded label, and one whose time has run out. Long ago it had been put upon The People by their colonizers. He meant it was time for The People to know who they really are; who they always have been.

I remember that when we reached Roy's Point there was a brief discussion about our gasoline supply. Our can was less than half full when we began the journey and we were concerned about getting out onto the lake and running out. Marv shook the red can and concluded that we would probably have enough to get back to dock but that it would be better to let the wind push us most of the way.

So he killed the engine and we began the quieter trip back. Immediately we both seemed to enjoy the silence. Now the welcome sound of the small waves was more noticeable, serving as a backdrop. Now the wind was with us, mildly blowing, changing its intensity now and then and at times gently shifting its direction. On my cheeks it was almost erotic—its gentle presence telling me I was out on the lake where it held sway.

Nodin, the wind, was warm when the Wet Dream moved out from under the shadows of the clouds and cool again when the sun was hidden by them. My awareness and enjoyment of the wind was heightened by these changes in temperatures, directions and intensities. The homes of the wind spirits are said to be located at the cardinal directions, but on that day with Uncle Marv they were out on Lake Superior, cavorting in the channel, reminding us that we were alive.

We made no bones about the fishing. At least today, I don't recall how we fussed over our lines and lures. Maybe we did change baits a few times, but I doubt it. I know that we got no strikes. Marv talked about how deep we were to fish and he checked this at least once, reeling in his line and attaching a sinker to take his bait down further. But except for these fussings, we left the rods alone. If we caught no fish that day, there would be other times.

As with the channel winds, gulls also were with us. These water birds are forms of life at home with all three primal places: the air, the land, the water. In my frame of mind that day they seemed nearly sacred—like Wenebozo to metamorphose, to move from one of these places to another easily, naturally. Gulls did not need a welded steel contraption to sit atop the water, nor to become airborne. We saw them on isolated small beaches, walking on the sand, or standing on those dark black boulders that often lie along the lake's shoreline. Some were sitting on the water, gently bobbing like grey and white plastic floats. Some flew close to us when we first entered the channel, slowly circling, their large heads bent forward and down to peer into the boat, looking for fish. But seeing none they soon lost interest and went back to their resting places on the waves.

I was struck by their cleanliness and I asked Uncle Marv about it. He said those with us that day seemed all to be adults. They had their white plumage, tipped with black and grey. No immature birds were near us and so we were treated to a plumed, neat brightness. Ours were of four colors: feet and beaks were a clean, bright orange that rivalled that of the Wet Dream; heads, breasts and most of the body were a crisp white; wing and tail feathers shared a bright grey, tipped with black. No colors blended, each keeping to its own area of the body.

When close up, these birds looked almost comical, their large blocky heads suggesting something from the film *Star Wars*. When landing in the water they would glide, and just before hitting the waves, their feet magically appeared. Then they would simply, in a quick little motion, sit on the water. Once this was accomplished they invariably adjusted their wings into what must have been comfortable positions, like someone sitting down in a theater—moving their shoulders a bit as they adjusted their buttocks to the seat.

Here was another community. These were beings who inhabited the coastlines of the earth, the boundaries between land and water. And they were equally at home in the air, gliding along, always like Marv, searching for something. That day on the lake I was awed by them. It must have been my time to contemplate the mystical. Never before had they seemed so hauntingly appropriate, so correct. They clearly were enjoying a comfortable fit with their world. Emissaries. Were they emissaries sent to teach? Foolishly I called, inviting them to come aboard the Wet Dream, but wisely, their black eyes turned away.

Water, wind, gulls, clouds, sunlight, shadows. Tree covered islands, green all over. Islands, like distant rounded worlds, plunked down onto the lake. We didn't really bring it all to words that day, but Uncle Marv and I were captivated by it all. There was nothing loudly important about it; just the two of us in that old smelly boat drifting on the lake. As it turned out, we were skunked—we caught no fish.

Finally, perhaps when satiated with the silence, Uncle Marv began talking again. Using his chin he pointed to Basswood and told about the day, long ago when a nephew of his swam all the way over to the island. Two miles or more. "Pinoke could swim," Marv said. "He was a strong one."

I asked why he did it and was told that there was no reason, really. It seems some of the young people were swimming at the old Red Cliff dock one day, and without any discussion this fellow announced he was going to swim to Basswood. After he started out, the others climbed into a wooden rowboat and rowed after him. They caught up, stayed with him, and after spending time on Basswood they all rowed back.

Then Marv started talking about the island on the other side of Basswood. Hermit Island. Known to non-Ojibwe for the recluse who used to live there, it is known at Red Cliff for another reason.

"That's where my grandpa buried his medicine," Marv said. We are all familiar with the story, but that day on the water I encouraged him to tell it again. I asked, "Just why did he do that?"

Marv held his gaze eastward to Basswood as if he was looking over or through the big island to Hermit. "I don't know," he began. "But they used to do that. The old ones, especially those who had no one to pass it on to."

Then he told the details of the family story again. His grandfather, like many elders long ago, had a personal medicine bag. These were deemed to be powerful—spiritually powerful—and to the wrong person they could be very dangerous. As with all medicine they had to be used correctly or, it seems, not used at all. There probably was a pipe in that bag.

In the late 1800's and early 1900's The People were under great pressure to give such things up. The village priests and nuns, especially, worked to discourage what they, like Allouez two or three hundred years ago, felt were "heathen" relics of the "pagan" past. Such objects, along with the beliefs and rituals they demanded, were "abominable." "Civilization" had come to the reservation.

So one day, as the story goes, Grandpa carefully placed his leather bag into its faded cloth wrapping and bundled it up. He walked down to the shoreline, stepped into a rowboat and began the long pull out to the islands.

I try to imagine what went through that old man's mind that day. And I try to imagine what goes through family members' minds today when they recall the story. No matter how I try to envision it, Marv's grandpa must have taken his time rowing over to Hermit. Occurring about a hundred years ago, the old man's solitary trip over the lake and back must have been deliberately done. Except for some words spoken over the burial, it must have been silent. Only the wind, the squeaking oarlocks, the sound of the dipping oars, and perhaps the birds were heard. The end of something as important as a way of life is not a little matter. The literature tells us such scenes were not unusual long ago. Medicine bags were personal items. While some may have been passed on to a younger person, an apprentice in some cases, most were probably ritually disposed of at the end of their holder's life. Their burial seems not to have been unusual. I wonder how many such pouches and bags are buried on Red Cliff's shoreline and on its islands. Surely they help make the land sacred and revered. When I see another new, overly done, large window-laden house going up on Madeline, one facing the lake, I think about this.

Uncle Marv was married twice. The first time it was to a young and beautiful Jewish-American woman from somewhere in Indiana. The summer they met he was working at a family resort in Northern Wisconsin where such people came to relax. He did general work around the dock and boat house, and at times would serve as a fishing guide. I have visions of the two of them out on the lake for an evenings row, Marv dazzling her with his stories.

But after less than a year, when the young couple came to the reservation and lived with Marv's parents in their small wood frame house, it became apparent to all that it was a mistake. I was told she soon left, heading south.

The second time worked much better. This time it was to a Native American woman from another Wisconsin tribe. They lived together in a few different places, until finally settling into an apartment in Milwaukee. We know of no children he fathered.

And Marv was also a veteran of the armed forces. In fact he was in two branches—the Marines and the Army. He joined the Marines at age sixteen, only to be found out several months after completing basic training and released. Then he joined the Army and spent time on the country's east coast near a large city. But he never talked much about this. The two photos of him in the two different uniforms sat for years on his mother's shelf in her living room. And later in his life he regularly used the medical services of the military installations in the Midwest.

As with his jobs and the military, Marv "stayed a while then disappeared." Restless like *Wenabozo,* he had something inside that kept him moving on. However, similarly, he had something inside that kept him coming home. I feel that finally, he never really left. While he was born at Red Cliff and raised there, upon reaching adulthood he hit the road. His long absences caused the next generations to be unfamiliar with him. In the later years he became one of the unknown on the reservation. Surely there were still those who did know him, and loved him, but for the large number of younger people he was not really known.

And this seemed to bother Marv, for he always identified with the community. It was his home to the end. He never relinquished his Ojibwe and his reservation identity. He was, I am certain, very proud of that.

In the times just before his health began to seriously falter, he would come home with an obvious passion to "do something," to work to improve things for the people. Once he ran for the Tribal Council but was easily defeated. But this did not deter his political ambitions. Many times he came to his sister's table for coffee only to start a harangue on treaty rights and lost lands. He could easily set things a-buzzin' with his talk. Sometimes people became upset with his persistence and drove him from the house. But a few weeks or months later, he would be back and it would all happen again.

There was the time when his troublesome persistence nearly became too much for me. My wife and I were living in Madison, Wisconsin, where I was in my last undergraduate year at the university. Marv showed up one day, obviously on one of his urban sojourns, and certainly in his cups. His mood was nostalgic. He talked about an uncle who was known to have carried the U.S. Mail from Bayfield to Superior, Wisconsin, in the 1800's.

This uncle was a family folk hero of sorts, said to have walked the seventy or so miles overland and in all seasons. There was no roadway between Bayfield and Superior in those days, so he used a foot trail. I recall that Uncle Marv's mother would relate how this relative would have a place in the woods at the halfway mark where he would kindle a fire, heat food and bed down for the night under the trees. It was said that he took a bottle of whisky along to help keep him going. Marv knew the state's historical archives were kept in Madison, and he asked that I take him to the large building so he could find the photos and documents about this uncle that were reputed to be stored there.

As he could be at those times, Marv was persistent so I cut my last class and took him over to the Historical Society. We climbed the wide marble steps and pulled open the heavy door. Walking up to the information desk, with slurred speech, Marv began asking to see "the pictures of my uncle." The female clerk was courteous, but perhaps from the smell of alcohol and the obviousness of the situation, she grew frustrated. I felt my own rising embarrassment and while Marv's voice started to grow louder, I recall glancing around for any advancing security guards. Without finding the pictures and documents, I ushered Uncle Marv out of the building.

Throughout most of his adult life, he might have felt quite powerless. He knew the stories of Sister Victoria, Sister Cordula, Sister This-n-that. He had experienced the rantings of the famous Father Oscar. He had been an altar boy. He knew the taste of the wafers and wine. His time was just before the advent of the open sweat lodge ceremonies on the reservation. He might have taken part in some of the earliest ones, especially in downstate ceremonies, but I do not know that he did. It would be interesting if he were here today to witness the recent flowering of traditionalism. Somehow I think that he might be troubled by it all, but then sometimes I am certain that he would be in the thick of it. Sometimes I imagine him dancing at the July 4th pow wow, and later joking about what long-gone Sister Victoria would say about it.

Occasionally, when out at the Frog Creek cabin, I relive the times he and I walked his little trap line along the slough and creek's shores. It saddens me when I realize how much he would have loved the cabin. It was built after his passing. Then there was the time my oldest son and I joined him in a rowboat to lift a small net he had set in the creek. We found several brook trout, but because he had failed to lift it in time—letting it go for a few days—the fish were soft and disintegrating. Once again he had been absent; was too late.

Several years ago, when on one of our weekend walkabouts at Red Cliff, we drove into the tribal campground at Raspberry. In those days, a large hand-painted, green and black tin sign nailed to two tall cedar posts stood out at the main road telling onlookers it was a tribal campground open only to tribal members.

Marv and I refreshed ourselves with the icy spring water spilling from the metal pipe rising from the ground near the campground's entrance, then walked the broken wooden "bridge" out to the long, pristine beach. We did not talk much on that walk. The usual beachcombing was done, the picking up of odd shaped pieces of driftwood, and the pocketing of any fishing net floats we found. We often went to that beach, as many Red Cliff people do, and I suspect they too are typically subdued when there. At Raspberry the big lake has a presence that only the very inept would not notice. Today the entire Raspberry area is considered to be one of the last places on the reserve that is still only for the Ojibwe people.

Coming back from the beach we walked through the campground, under the red pines. I had my camera and was shooting nearly everything in sight and Marv lost interest in my companionship. He wandered off by himself. Meanwhile, a car with a boat on a trailer had driven into the campground and was backed up to the landing at the river on the campground's west side. I was preoccupied with my picture-taking and did not pay much attention to Marv as he strolled over to the two men who began to unfasten the boat.

I assumed the men were from Red Cliff and when Marv starting talking with them I paid more attention. Still seventy-five feet or more distant I could, nevertheless, understand what was being said. After the usual greetings I heard Marv ask if they were tribal members.

"No," one of the men replied. "We have one of those houses over there." He was referring to the piece of township land way over on the cliffs on the distant side of Raspberry Bay, perhaps a mile away. This parcel had been portioned into a few small lots by a developer after World War II, and while most plots were now owned by Red Cliff people, a few were still in the hands of outsiders.

"Well," Marv went on. "Didn't you read the sign out there? This is for tribal members only."

By then I had started walking toward the landing and I could feel the surprise registered by the two men. There was a long pause before Marv went on.

"There are docks in Bayfield for you. Go use them. You can't put your boat in here," he said.

I did not hear a response, but after more silence the two reattached the trailer's lines to the boat—it was still on the trailer—and entered their car. Its engine was quickly started. As they slowly pulled away from the landing and made the loop under the pines, Marv and I met.

"Holy shit!" I remember saying to him. "That was beautiful!"

He was silent as he watched the car make the loop. Then as it came to the place near where we stood it stopped and one of the men opened a door and stepped out. He walked a few feet toward us and asked, looking at Uncle Marv, "What's your name?"

"Never mind," he replied. "I got my Tribal I. D. card. You don't."

The fellow did not say more. He turned and walked back to the car and it drove out of the campground.

We began to walk back to our car, apparently feeling our walk was over. I could not hide my pleasure and I recall telling Uncle Marv how good it was to have watched him run those fellows out.

"Hey, they can read. The sign says 'Tribal Members Only.'" Then he went on with obvious disgust in his voice. "Some people have been doin' this for years. They think they can run all over Red Cliff, hunt and fish anywhere, set traps, use our beaches. Enough of that shit. This is ours."

Over the years, whenever I have the opportunity to tell this story, I invariably add how Uncle Marv grew in size that day. "He was absolutely wonderful," I like to add.

The southerly wind kept us moving through the channel but because of its movement we were sometimes blown off course so the engine had to be started a few times. We began to worry again, about the gas. And the sun had started its western descent. There were no lights on the Wet Dream.

Then, with the approaching dusk, the winds died down. We finally had to use the engine to cover the half mile or so left and deciding our fishing was over, I reeled in both lines while Marv handled the motor. One line came in easily but when bringing mine in I either reeled too fast or had a strike because suddenly something let go and my reeling became much easier. Perhaps the combination of the increased speed of the boat and my fast reeling did it. I pulled my line in without its large red and white spoon.

"Hey," I shouted above the now louder moan of the engine. "We had a strike!" I held the end of my lure-less line up for Marv to see. He puckered his lips in the Ojibwe fashion, and raising his eyes with wrinkled brow, he pointed with his chin to the end of the line. Later we told the family that at least we got a strike, or that at least it could have been a strike.

I remember that, as we approached the marina, my wife was seen walking down the hill to check on us. It was getting dark now and she was pleased to see that we were getting off the lake safely. I handed her our two little inexpensive rods and tackle boxes as she told how we were to hurry. It was getting late and bingo would be starting soon.

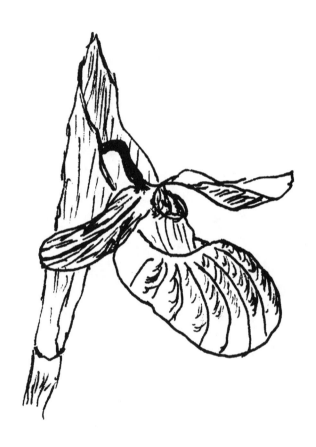

The Flowers
of Red Cliff

*If there's an art to being human and
comfortable, part of it involves learning
to get quiet.*
— **William Kittredge, 1999**

When on the reservation in spring, I go looking for flowers. After years of searching, of asking the elders, of leafing through old books, I am finding them. They are everywhere. In the proper seasons, the reservation is a-bloom.

These are *northern* flowers, hinting of the Arctic. They tell of long winters and sudden, vibrant, forceful springs. A few, like autumn's goldenrod, offer a last hurrah, a deep, golden thrust of life before the onset of winter's killing cold. A flower is a mechanism for ensuring ongoing life. At Red Cliff, most must be found quickly, lest their blooms be withered and gone. In such a place, it could be said that the important matter of reproduction is sometimes handled in the blink of an eye.

Lying along the southern shore of Lake Superior, Red Cliff is in a mixed biome. The big lake is split into two plant regions— its northern half assigned to the Northeastern Coniferous Forest Region, and its southern half made up of this same region but with an overlay of the Eastern Deciduous Forest Region.

So, while generally the lake's northern shore holds a coniferous forest, the southern shore holds both conifers and hardwoods. This makes for a complicated floral mix at Red Cliff. Majestic red oaks can be found competing with balsams, hemlocks, and cedars. Maples and tall green ash trees likewise. When moving along a forest path, it seems to me that the conifers are more at home here, but then I come upon an oak or a maple or ash, seemingly feeling just as comfortable. In some of the reservation lowlands, black spruces tell of the Northern Boreal Forest, but then there are those groves of oaks that hark of a more southern clime. Red Cliff can be difficult to categorize, to come to grips with. In its diversity and contradictions lies its richness.

Botany was my second declared undergraduate major. The first was forestry. My childhood and youth had not included the word botany. This academic awareness was initially planted by the clever hands of Dr. Franklin Lane over in Ashland. In 1959, at Northland College, I took his introductory botany course. I have never forgotten it. We met in wonderfully old Woods Hall, now torn down. Its large, aging, ground level windows would flood my laboratory workstation with warm sunlight.

Dr. Newton Bobb, still on campus, appeared in class now and then to give a presentation of interest to him. Today, ghostlike in my memory, I still see his quiet figure in lab-coat, down a hallway, disappearing into an office. In those fleeting times I saw him, I mixed the young man in the college logo in which he stands in the forest with an axe in his hands, with the real, aged Professor Bobb. The logo depicts a scene from a photograph taken nearly one hundred years ago.

But I left Northland College, transferring to the University of Wisconsin at Madison. This drastic change was made for matters of money and a youthful restlessness. At Madison I held a student job in the herbarium, again enjoying plants, their dusty, dry stems crackling as I labored over a years-long mapping project. It was there I discovered an old tiny, thin book by

Dr. Norman Fassett entitled *Spring Flora of Wisconsin*. A quiet little joy, it led me on along my botanical path.

All this was interrupted by romance, family, and anthropology. But this diversion never really took me away from flowers. In my study of anthropology I was again amidst them. When I came to the reservation, there they were, at Red Cliff, along its eighteen miles of wooded shoreline, in its sloughs, bogs, woodland clearings, under its forest canopy. A treasure to behold. And they are still here, forty years later.

Each year I shoot rolls and rolls of film, trying to capture their beauty. The jack-in-the-pulpit behind the cabin, Aunt Rose's trailing arbutus in Raspberry Campground. Pussy willows, wild peas, thimbleberry and blooming white cedar trees. For years I naively assumed that some reservation members did not see the flowers. It seemed to me these people rushed past them as they played out their hurried lives. Usually there was no talk of flowers, no passing comment on their quiet presence. The Ojibwe people I knew were more interested in *people* than wild flowers.

If I did call someone's attention to a small white star fire beside a cabin trail I usually was given a second of time, perhaps a polite nod of the head, a cursory glance. Then hurrying along I might hear a comment on "how pretty those fields of flowers were at 'the orchards.'" This was a reference to the domestic varieties grown and marketed by John Hawser of Hawser's Orchards on the hills north of Bayfield, just southwest of Red Cliff.

To the people, the forest's flowers were, it seemed to me, *just there*. I wondered if they actually saw them. But it was *I* that was not paying attention. I was reading the people in *my* way, not in theirs.

In those years I was gushing over the wild flowers. Maybe, like a boy with a new toy, I was possessed by my fascination with them. Now, the same esthetic emotion is still alive in me, but is seasoned with years of living. Perhaps I have learned, as environmentalist writer William Kittredge says, "to get quiet" in the awesome presence of Nature. Perhaps the Ojibwe people have taught me this: not to gush, not to analyze something to the extreme. Maybe they even are saying not to take all those damn pictures. Maybe they are telling me to just let the flowers be.

I have been taught that the reservation's wild flowers are all part of a bigger reality, one that naturally transcends human foibles, goes beyond, even the noise of Bayfield, Washburn, and Ashland.

But I need to pause and ask what the word flower refers to. What is a flower? And what do we mean when we way someone, or something, is flowering, is blooming? Once again, it is dangerous to stop and ponder the very words we use as we share our lives. Such an undertaking can show us not just the arbitrary nature of our word choices (a language community can choose any sound, or combination of sounds, for any meaning) but finally, when pushing this, we must realize the struggle humans have to adequately describe their experiences. In times of greatest meaning we can "be at a loss for words." We can be "left speechless." Sometimes language is not good enough. It fails us, and we can only express ourselves in shouts or physical actions of raw emotion. Perhaps in such peak times we are like the plants, like the flowers. Perhaps we become quiet.

So, here I will use flower, in its various grammatical forms, in a very broad manner. I will open the concept up, take a writer's license with it. To me all plants "flower," give issue. Even the reservation's tiniest, those we seldom ponder, "flower" as they reproduce. The soft, lush mosses, with their spores, "flower." The bushes and shrubs, the grasses—all the diverse forms of life in the reservation's meadows, clearings, creek bottoms, "flower."

Those living on the sandy beaches of Sand Bay, Eagle Bay, Raspberry Bay, Red Cliff Creek Bay, Buffalo Bay, and all the little swatches of sand between these big bays, "flower." The ancient Equistrium, the "horsetails" we find here and there, "flower." The thick alderbrush that can line a creek and in its stubborn way can block our passage, "flowers." The hardwoods—in their several varieties—bring forth tiny little blossoms and "flower." The cones of the hemlocks, cedars, balsams and pines, come forth to reproduce. And the delightful resins of these trees can fill the forest with perfume.

In an often bewildering way, the land at Red Cliff comes forth to bloom. Its many perfumes scent the air, are taken up by the winds.

Like all forms of life, plants are caught up in the tugs and pulls of evolution. Their existence, like ours, is processual, enmeshed in the flow of all things. They, too, move along the complex pathway of steadfastness and change. Not all forms of life last forever.

With this in mind, I am interested when my forty-five-year-old botany textbook tells me one of the reservation's plants is on its way out, or, as the author claims, "is traveling the road to extinction." This is genus *Equisetum*, the "horsetails." Horsetails are those small, sometimes translucent, segmented, tubular plants found on beaches, in bogs and along creeks. Their numbers peaked between 270 and 300 million years ago. We cannot comprehend such a length of time. We are told that ever since they have been fighting a losing battle, albeit a lengthy one. It is taking a long time for this plant to die.

Red Cliff's horsetails are true survivors. To some viewers, perhaps, they are seen as living fossils. If they are dying out, they are doing a good job of hanging on. They reside throughout the entire reservation. Written with a material use, my botany text goes on to say that "Living species of horsetails have virtually no economic value in human life." However, we are told that in their present form, due to their tough exteriors, they are used to scour "cooking pots and pans and floors," but that this use has "almost disappeared except in remote rural areas." (Domestic servants? Day laborers? Remote rural areas? Our horsetails conjure up interesting images.)

To economic botanists, the lowly horsetail, while serving little purpose to us when alive, is more useful after death. Some of their bodies make up our valuable coal beds. Apparently their contribution is in their death.

A Red Cliff plant of much interest to me is the tamarack. This Algonkian word rings with antiquity. In Latin called a larch, the tamarack is a coniferous tree that is deciduous. Its soft green needles grow in tufts instead of being singly attached along a stem's length. In fall these soft green "leaves" turn a bright yellow—their autumnal glow matching that of the aspens—then they detach and fall. (Deciduous is Latin for "fall.")

Somehow, the tamarack stands between the two great classes of seed plants recognized in the Western world: Class *Angiospermae* and Class *Gymnospermae*. It straddles both categories, one foot in each. In doing so it reminds us that here our intellectual categories are "artificial," imposed onto a deeper commonality. It raises the interesting scene wherein these categories are drummed into the mind of the schoolchild as absolute knowledge, when finally, they would be better taken as knowledge specific to a certain community, to a particular society.

Tamaracks can be classified differently in different parts of the world. They can be seen—be understood—in different ways. There is no one way to classify, to make sense of, a tamarack tree. On a walk in the Red Cliff woods you can suddenly have the mind-jarring experience that here the Linnaen scheme of things, the "universal taxonomic system" of plant classification used in the "world botanical community," can be set aside, not recognized as the starting point as you attempt to comprehend what you see before you.

One of the most fragrant trees in the Red Cliff woods is the aspen. Both *sawtooth* and *quaking* aspens are ubiquitous on the reservation. To me, the "lowly" aspen sits on high. It epitomizes The Northland. For long considered a trash tree, it is now valued for its importance in making paper pulp. In the ideology of the marketplace, the aspen has found its place.

In his book entitled *The Music of Failure,* Minnesota writer Bill Holm offers a more poetic image of the aspen. Holm tells of sitting high in the Rockies, under an aspen tree that is being made "musical" by the wind moving through its quaking leaves. He suggests that the wind is trying to blow the leaves off the tree, but is failing. Yet in this failure we are given a wonderful music. His book goes on to give us vignettes from the lives of several acquaintances of his, people who might, in the arrogant "wisdom" of certain parts of the world, be viewed as failures. Holm suggests that the lives of these people have been anything but failures. Among other things, they have given us wonderful music.

Quaking aspens are found in western states at higher altitudes, in locations that climate-wise are like those in more northern latitudes. The tree seems to love the cold, at least below the extreme northern tree line. At my suburban home, when I want to be projected into "The North," I snap an aspen twig and chew it, the pungent perfume transporting me to the Red Cliff woods, the place from whence my suburban tree came.

How to describe the smell of aspen? Sweet? Woody and wild? Like the meat of a tough old male deer tastes? When it comes to attempts to describe smells we can only go to comparisons. We say something smells like something else. Finally, we might assign to the aspen its own smell. In a wonder-filled tautology, we can say that the aspen smells like aspen. Leave it at that.

Often the first species to rush into a patch of clear-cut woods, aspens crowd together like a flock of schoolchildren waving little flags at a passing president. Growing quickly, in only thirty-five years or so, they are ready for "harvest." To me they are "harvested" all through their lives—from sprout to sapling to adult. Their entire life cycle is "a crop" to be harvested by eye, nose, ear, touch, and taste. They can fill our imagination with their presence.

Labrador tea, with its leathery leaves and their soft suede-like undersides is another plant of the north. Its perfume graces numerous sloughs on the reservation. Wintergreen, in both its waxy leaf and little red berry form, is a delight to chew, to swallow, to digest. It makes a pleasantly aromatic jam to be spread onto hot buttered toast in deep January. A species of wild peppermint is well known by reservation residents. When coming into an isolated clearing in the proper season, you can be treated to its aroma. Like a cleansing expurgator, it can clear your lungs, and mind. It is an old favorite at Red Cliff. Wild ginger, *namapin,* is just as well known. It is common on the forest floor, and used for mouth and throat ailments. And there are many more, more plants that give themselves to the people. The woods are full of medicine.

Several years ago, my youngest son and I had spent a day in the woods, peeling balsam logs to be used in building a cabin. We labored in the heat of the June day, dousing our exposed skin with mosquito repellant, wiping our sweaty brows. To use the old cliche, it was a labor of love, for we both eager anticipated the rising of the cabin walls. At the end of the afternoon, when we had to pack up our tools and leave the woods for an evening family meal, we stopped in the little grocery store that stood at the edge of one of the reservation's housing projects for pop. Upon entering the little shop we greeted Rosemary, one of the proprietors, and she greeted us back. Then she said, "You guys were peeling balsam."

Zhingob. Balsam fir. *Wenebozo uses zhingob.* The legends tell of it's perfume. It is better known than other conifers for its resinous pungency. The balsam has that "Christmas tree" scent. Another tree sometimes disregarded by loggers, balsam trees are left standing when other species are cut and removed. Neglected at times, it can be subjected to the humiliation of having lower boughs snapped off for wreaths. The balsam tree submits to the indignity, and is left standing in the crowded woods to recover in time.

Red Cliff is covered with balsams. We use their boughs for making tea. This dark green tree, emerald in its conical beauty, stays bright, like the other conifers, all winter. It toughs out this hard season, refusing to drop its leaves. In this way, its bloom is constant, with us in all seasons. It is one of our most treasured flowers.

Two other significant reservation conifers are the spruces and hemlocks. For years, people searched the woods for young spruces, which were popular, naturally grown Christmas trees. Today their numbers seem limited on the reserve. Still, coming upon a spruce in the woods, whether big or small, is a pleasure to see. Usually more symmetrical than balsams, and often growing to heights that far surpass the balsam, the spruce can be a monumental tree.

It is the hemlocks that perhaps have a more interesting story. Hemlocks with their short, flat, deep green needles, their tiny brown cones, and their mature brown bark that is so dark it looks to be a step away from black, are scattered throughout the reservation. At first not thought worthy, they were usually bypassed by the lumbermen. Another "trash" tree, many stood until the more valuable species were depleted. But then the speculators came again with their saws to "harvest" what had been left behind. A second coming. A second cutting.

Some large, massive hemlocks stood at Red Cliff until World War II days. But most were cut earlier for their bark. Sometimes the wood was discarded, left to rot. An ignoble way to treat a noble tree. The bark was sought for its tannin, used in the leather tanning industry.

Recently a tribal elder told me how when he was a youngster, his mother would send him out into the forest for *nagek,* the dried bark of downed hemlocks. He piled it atop his sled and brought loads of it back to her sugar camp. She treasured it as fuel under her syrup finishing kettles for its low, even flame.

But it's enough for me just to be amongst the hemlocks, to see them. I love to take a bough in my hands to study its short needles, its tiny brown cones. And I love to walk into a thick hemlock grove. The dark trees have a quietude, a history. Their groves sometimes provide winter sanctuaries for deer. They yard up under them.

Two more Red Cliff conifers that "bloom" are the red and white pines. More familiar than the cedar trees, it is the white pines that paid an awful price in the great lumbering era. True behemoths, white pines towered over the other trees. And they fell quickly, to the axe and saw, to be dragged, pulled, floated and otherwise hauled to the mills. Today relatively few white pines stand in the Northern Wisconsin woods.

Some are found at Red Cliff. There are attempts to bring them back. Today, when a forty or eighty-acre piece of forest is clear-cut, a large white pine is left standing as a seed tree in hopes its seeds with spring forth. Such a tree, out in a devastated plot of woods, looks like a lone survivor standing dazed in a bombed village.

Last year one of the two large white pines before our Frog Creek cabin suddenly dropped its needles. Now dead, perhaps from a rust disease, it would make an excellent spot for a nest built by the eagles that fish the creek. We watch. We wait.

Red pines, with their quick growth, are found at Red Cliff. In the 1960's old clearings were planted with the little seedlings. Some of the clearings were former farm fields from the late 1800's, a time when the people were told to give up "the chase" and "settle down." Today these red pine plantations stand, lush with their long, hard needles, emerging as thick groves of greenery that tell of man's intervention.

Among all these conifers is one more: the white cedar. Preferring the wet lowlands, these straight grained, smooth barked, fragrant trees were cut for use as fence posts. Loads after loads of white cedar bolts were hauled from the Red Cliff woods. Today these trees rarely reach maturity, often falling to the chainsaw when reaching post size. But in a few places the big ones are still found. Some are too big for a grown man to reach around. When in the presence of such giants, humans grow silent.

This has been called the sacred tree of the Ojibwe. Many of the world's cultures have sacred trees. These plants play pivotal roles in the people's origins statements. In Ojibwe culture the cedar is the axis mundi. Truly the center of the earth, it appears as an important person in ceremonies. Swatches of boughs are kept in houses and renewed regularly. The essence of cedar, its aroma and smoke, is breathed in deeply. Its sweet, fragrant, bouquet cleanses. The tree is respected.

There are other flowers at Red Cliff. Not native to Lake Superior country, they were brought by newcomers. Invaders like purple loosestrife are seen today, making inroads in ditches and lagoons. It is said they are a serious threat for they quickly replace native plants that normally dwell in such places. Others, like the showy roadside lupines photographed by tourists and so often painted by artists, are sometimes sought out, are even planted by some reservation residents.

Then, in season, we can find abandoned home sites when old rhubarb plants bloom, their white flowery spikes standing like surveyors' markers. And domestic apple trees gone wild, all thick and unkempt, bloom in a wonderful wildness here and there throughout the woods, telling of dreams that have run their course. Now and then other flower-garden blooms can be seen: clumps of old domestic roses, bright blue splashes of bee-balm, and white, fragrant clusters of an ancient jonquil, so tough and tenacious, coming back year after year. Often these flowering plants stand beside the dainty blossoms of chokecherry and wild plum "brush." True juxtapositions, such scenes tell of the coming together of the tame and the wild.

Today, with the desire for wooden decks attached to houses, we find a bright proliferation of "window box" flowers on the reservation. Huge showy petunias, with blooms draping their green foliage, and the incessant colors of impatiens, so common in cities are easily come upon. Usually forced with chemical potions, these flowers can spring forth with a profusion of growth and bloom that is, perhaps, mind-boggling—their growth sometimes said to be a miracle.

Flowers are part of funerals on the reservation. The formal floral designs of regional florists stand beside displayed caskets, and later might be laid to mold and decay atop a new grave. These artificial arrangements pull us into the mainstream, as they narrow us. Their ostentatiousness is deafening. Their roar, finally, empty. Greenhouse flowers, forced under glass, shipped in from distant places, places afar, maybe even Chile. Invaders again. No waft of aroma. All show. Yet, they are so beautiful, so sought after, and so expensive. In an interesting way these funeral flowers have been said to be more dead than the dead. They are not of the land, of the Lake Superior shoreline.

Flowers are important symbols. Their fleeting moments of life are like all life—transient. Here, then gone. It is suggested that 40 thousand years ago Neanderthal people were sometimes buried with woven mats of flowers. To the Neanderthals fragrant flowers, apparently, offered some hope of a beyond. And several years ago, on Madeline Island, only three miles from Red Cliff, while excavating for a golf course, somebody found ancient human remains, still wrapped in a roll of birch bark. In old times this bark was used as a covering, a "blanket" for lodges, and yes, for bodies. The people wrapped their dead in the bark of the white birch tree.

And then, at Red Cliff, there are plastic "flowers." These monstrosities have become part of our lives. They are hung on kitchen walls, stuck in outdoor flower boxes, placed at grave sites. We even use them to celebrate death. In spring, on Memorial Day, a wreath of black plastic flowers might be placed at the base of the big wooden cross that stands in the center of the reservation's cemetery. Some, in appropriate colors, are fastened together in small renditions of the American flag and displayed at the heads of graves. At Red Cliff, as in "greater" United States society, plastic flowers seem to be everywhere.

Plastic has become part of our lives, even, in some cases, part of our bodies. We live with plastic. In some cases we live because of it. But try as I might to understand the phenomenon of plastic flowers, I fail to grasp it. Perhaps it is true what is said of them: they represent eternity.

Last June, I found two of the greatest treasures of the Northwoods. On my way out to one of the reservation's beaches I turned off the path, onto a faint trail, one rarely used, and stepped into the woods. I looked for and found the bed of pink moccasin flowers I knew were growing in that spot. These orchids—also called lady slippers—stood in the cool shade of a grove of red pines. They were in full bloom. I found a bare spot amongst them and sat down upon the dry pine needles. It was good to pause and be with them. This time I took no pictures, tried not to stare. I did not want to intrude, even did not want to think about them. I came just to be there, to be in their presence. We are told flowers are not conscious, not aware of themselves, but, anthropomorphizing or not, I felt they welcomed my presence. They let me warm myself by their fire.

Later, out on the beach, I found the delicate wild rose. Protected by a line of tall grasses and other bushes, they were back from the water, standing along the line of vegetation at the high water mark. Nearly hidden amidst the profusion of their branches was a metal post that marked a "property" line. Real estate. Even here, I thought, on the shore of Gichigami, were boundaries. But these wild roses recognized no such lines. They easily spread their roots, gave rise to their greenery with its short but still sharp thorns, and in season, issued pink buds that opened into dainty fragrant flowers. They were grounded in the earth as they lifted their blooms upward to the sky and outward to the big lake.

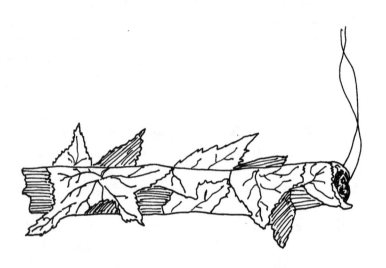

Holding Court

Something passes more than I am
aware of. A truth that goes on.
— Diane Glancy, 1992

Lizzy Roy held court that day. It had been a long time, but there she was, seated at the kitchen table, her offspring around her. She is a matriarch of sorts, outliving all her siblings, her husband, and three of her six children. That day several years ago, for a few hours at least and at 91, she was still able to command an audience—was still in charge.

One of her granddaughters drove over to Washburn that morning for a visit at the nursing home, and found her crying in her room. Between sobs she kept muttering, "Take me home, take me home." So there she was—maroon calico cotton dress, wheelchair, artificial leg and large tan vinyl purse—pushed up to her place at the head of the table.

It was a familiar scene. I recall how for years on weekends, when a subtle festive air permeated the village, she would walk to this house to visit her daughter and be with her grandchildren. Lizzy would finish her own household chores early on Saturday morning—her small wood framed house was just a quarter mile up the road—and come to sit and talk, to be part of the activity that was often present there.

Coffee was poured, the chipped ceramic sugar bowl—with the faded red rose on each side—was brought from the cupboard, and the blue and white can of Pet condensed milk with its yellowed puncture holes emerged from the refrigerator. A stack of unevenly cut slices of homemade wheat bread, an end of mild yellow cheese, and perhaps a partial pink ring of course-ground bologna would be set onto the table. She spent hours talking, laughing, and generally overseeing the activities of the family those mornings. This is an old custom at Red Cliff.

Like royalty, I thought, Lizzy would walk into the small four-room house, take her seat and hold court. Over the years she emerged as a stable leader who was loved by her followers. She had the oratorical skills of a natural storyteller and was eager to use them. If she had been born a generation or two earlier she would have told of Wenebozo, the Ojibwe culture hero, and how in his foolishness he taught the people how to live. But Lizzy was born in 1892, when Christianity weighed heavily upon the people as they were expected to live like their white neighbors.

So her stories were of the times of logging camps and lumber mills, of the great Hinckley fire, of men who went off to fight in wars far overseas, of women who often stayed home to labor—to struggle to raise their young. And she told of powerful priests with their followings of supplicating nuns, of the first automobiles to come from town, coughing up the trails that cut through the wooded hills leading to the reservation.

We listened to her tell so easily of things from another time and we struggled to grasp what it was like then, to understand her frame of reference. Like her, we lived in the present and anticipated the future but she knew more than us, for she came from somewhere we had never been and her voice called us to join her, to see those times again.

Her stories were of people and how their relationships could often take humorous turns. How we would listen and watch and enjoy! How, at times, we would laugh with her. Arms gesticulating, she would spread her love for the family outward like gentle waves rolling up on clean sandy shores.

Lizzy was immensely Christian. With chin-determined pride she would tell of her years of devotion to the string of priests and nuns that, over her lifetime, flowed through the village like soldiers sent to their tour of duty at the frontier. For years and years she attended Mass daily, not just on Sunday, or worse yet, as she said, "only at Christmas and Easter like some people." Yet with all her modern ways she retained a tie with the past, with her ancestors.

One of them she said, came from Michigan. It was her paternal grandfather. For some unknown reason he was taken in, she claimed, "by a black family" that gave him their family name. And it was these kind people who, she insisted, "taught him how to use a fork."

Several years ago, when she was still living in her immaculately clean house, I stopped to visit on my way home from the trout-fishing hole on Chicago Creek. We were in the midst of a string of overcast days, and the weather affected her mood, for I found her pensively seated at her table, alone.

After expressing pleasure at the size of my catch, and after laying the two trout I gave her into a pan of clear, cool water in the sink, she talked of change, of how the tourists were appearing with increasing regularity. "Yes," she said sadly, "everything is changed. Even the *manidoog* are gone."

At the time, to me, this was a startling revelation. This woman was a Christian, who in past years when I naively tried to get her to talk about "the old religion" would clam up with a downturned mouth. I recall one occasion when at a small workshop in the tribal arts and crafts center she was asked by the presenter about some old Ojibwe belief, and she responded with dismay, saying, "Huuuf—I don't know about anything like that. I'm a Christian."

However, I do not believe she really felt that the *manidoog* had deserted her, those spirits of the Ojibwe, for only three years previous, when at an outdoor ordination ceremony held on the reservation for a local youth who was becoming a Catholic priest, she asked to be wheeled up to a small fire and circled around it, depositing a pinch of tobacco in the process.

The fire was part of a ritual led by a contingent of young

Ojibwe who, although not professing to be Christians, had been asked to participate in the celebration. None of her children and few of her grandchildren went with her. At the time, paradoxically it seemed to me, she appeared to be suddenly free from the modern restraints that held her offspring tight. They stood quietly at the periphery of the event, under the deep green large spruce trees at the edge of the grassy clearing.

Today such ceremonial fires—and much more—are openly seen on the reservation. But back then, on the day of the ordination, they were something relatively recent. While over the years they had gone on in private, away from the public's eye, I felt it was quite unusual to witness such a public display. I see now that it was the beginning of something that has been quietly growing ever since. And I want to think that Lizzy's prescience that day was another of her teachings. Even accepting her stern stand on Christianity and other outside "modern" things, perhaps paradoxically she was telling us of the future.

Lizzy represents a generation or two of Ojibwe people who felt the brunt of change. Throughout most of her earlier years the bulk of the political power was centered outside the reservation. While claims of sovereignty and treaty rights have an ancient history at places like Red Cliff, these voices were generally muted in the days of her childhood, youth, and adulthood. It was only near the end of her years—in the 1960's and 1970's especially—that she began to witness the resurgence of an open expression of traditional Ojibwe ways. For a person who lived a lifetime being told that "the Old Way was dead" it might be difficult to witness such a resurgence. After all, many native people made conscious decisions to give up the old and accept the new. Were they wrong? In some cases bridges were burned. How could it be possible to go back? And furthermore, "Weren't we told that The New is the better way? Do you mean to say that all the time this was a lie? Do you mean that The Old is better?"

Yet, for people like Lizzy, there must be an overwhelming feeling of joyous wonder at the resurgence of the Old Way. This is the way the ancestors lived.

This joyful surprise in the return of traditionalism can be seen in two other incidents I recall at Red Cliff. Lizzy was involved in both. The first occurred in the early 1970's when one of her grandsons stopped cutting his hair. He had been attending a downstate university and she had not seen him for some time. Then he showed up one day with a long black braid running down his back. To add an exclamation point on his statement, he wore a black, wide brimmed wool "Billy Jack" hat. I recall how Lizzy's mouth fell when first seeing him.

The very next day she came down to her daughter's house with a colorful yarn sash that she made the night before. I remember when she handed it to the grandson, saying, "Here. If you want to dress that way, you have to wear this."

The other incident occurred at my suburban home. Lizzy had come down for a visit, as she would do now and then before her health failed. I had a copy of a book about Minnesota Ojibwe people by the White Earth writer Gerald Vizenor. On its cover was a large photo of a wizened Ojibwe elder. His face was covered with wrinkles, his chins with white bristles, and he wore a floppy felt hat—the sort sometimes worn by older reservation people in the past.

Lizzy took the book and again her mouth fell in disbelief. After drawing in a mouthful of air, she said, "Just think. They put a picture of an old man like that on the cover of a book!" To her books represented something important and nowhere in her past had she ever seen an old Ojibwe man's face on a book's cover. Times were changing.

But these little anecdotal stories are easy to read. They show her obvious attachment to the old belief system. The importance of her remarks about the *manidoog* are clear. However, I feel that, like other humans, Lizzy showed her true feelings at times when she chose not to use speech. Several such instances rest in my memory, each showing her attachment to the old ideologies and her tight grip on the land. Once, way back in 1962 when Marlene and I brought our newly born son to Red

Cliff to meet the family, we all went out to Raspberry Bay for a cookout. This was the old-fashioned cookout, held right on the big sandy beach, not back in the village on someone's wooden deck attached to their house. This was the time we erected a small teepee of saplings, wrapped blankets around it and secured the baby inside, suspended in a cloth "swing." The wind was strong that day and such an old structure was a safe place for the little one to sleep.

With the baby at rest, the women prepared a boiled dinner on the beach. My old photos show Lizzy sitting prominently before the fire, large wooden spoon in hand, tending the boiling kettle. She sat facing the big lake, its waves only about fifteen feet away. I recall how she quietly enjoyed the day. She did not need speech to show it. It was something she was very familiar with and something she deeply loved. She had prepared a meal on Red Cliff's beaches many times in her life.

That day it seemed to me that much of her time was spent simply looking at the lake, beach, sky, and islands. She remarked now and then about how some of the nearby shoreline plants would be used in the past, and she related incidents when she was young. She told of the good times when she and her husband used to, as she said, "live in our shack at Frog Bay." At one time I remember her saying, "Those were good times. I really liked it at that place. Frog Bay is the prettiest place at Red Cliff."

There was another time, in early spring when the ice was almost ready to break up. I had been exploring along the shoreline at Buffalo Bay and upon returning to the house found she had walked down for a visit. I extolled what I considered the wonders of the ice and then I admonished those in the kitchen for "wasting" such a beautiful day by just sitting at the table "having coffee." She looked at me, forgiving by passion, and quietly began a short discourse of her own. She quickly told of the changes in the winter's ice once warm weather came, how its structure began to take other forms. "Sometimes," she went on, "it gets just like long, clear nails that break free and tinkle like little silver bells when you reach in for a handful. I used to like to suck on those cold nails, to hear them break in my mouth as I ate them."

Here was knowledge gained from a lifetime of living by *Gichigami*. My experiences paled in meaning compared to hers. While I merely told of my excitement with a new discovery, she offered a quiet wisdom. I see now that at such times Lizzy was sharing her knowledge about the spirituality of Lake Superior and its surroundings. I could tell her nothing new about it. She rarely talked of the *manidoog*, but when she did speak of the land, and more importantly, when she moved about out in it, her behavior exuded a deep conviction in its power. After all, it was not proper to speak openly of the spirits. This remains a strong Ojibwe rule.

Perhaps one more such story needs to be told. This was something I never had the opportunity to witness, but my wife loves to tell of it, especially in spring. Marlene lived in Lizzy's house for several of her youthful years. In Ojibwe culture it is customary for a daughter to send one of her youngsters to live with their grandparents, especially if they are alone. It is easy to understand the purpose here—how the older couple may need the labor of a youngster in the house, and importantly, how such a custom affords an arena for the elders to bring teachings to the child.

The relevant story here is that, in spring, Lizzy would take walks in the nearby woods. This is somewhat unusual since, I believe, in traditional Ojibwe culture the woods are said to be "the domain of the man" while the household is "the domain of the woman." It seems if one or the other person spent too much time alone in the domain of the opposite gender that something was awry, not "normal." Yet, Marlene insists that Lizzy would take such walks, and take the young granddaughter along. Lizzy would welcome the coming of another spring on these walks, and a major element of them was to smoke a cigarette while ambling along amongst the trees. But it was not a typical cigarette. This was an offering of another kind. Although Lizzy

usually had a supply of real cigarettes on hand, on such walks
......she would select the best of last season's dried maple leaves,
carefully roll a few into a "cigarette," light it with a wooden
match and, as she slowly walked through the woods, smoke the
rolled leaves.

I see something spiritual in this. Here was a woman who
had been taught with all due determination, to be "civilized."
While walks in the spring woods are not unusual, such a walk
by an Ojibwe elder in the 1940's in the woods beside Lake Superior, on land that The People have occupied for over 300 years,
does suggest an added meaning. She chose not to use the modern store-bought cigarette. Ritually, she made her own from
the leaves of the forest. She did it the Old Way.

I still marvel at her memory, but more importantly, at her
intelligence. That large, dark woman who, as a six-year-old child,
started grade school in 1898, knowing very little English, had
an insight into the workings of the human world that is beyond
most of us. This was always clear to us, but made especially
poignant on those Saturday mornings when she was at our table,
talking. At those times, the kitchen was often filled with the
pulsation of summertime Saturday mornings. Youngsters came
and went, slamming the screen door behind them.

But then her age took its toll. Diabetes finally became extreme. The stubborn sores on her foot refused to leave, spreading to the lower leg. It was removed. Weakened and disheart-
ened, she decided the doctors were right. She entered the nursing home. There, after a year of living in an antiseptic room
with a withered, bedridden roommate who could not talk—a
year of increasingly infrequent weekend trips home—another
blow struck. This time it was a mild heart attack. Lizzy was
failing, her lifelong glory leaving. Her long gleaming black hair
was now short, bristly and white. Her physical strength was
moving on. She slept a lot, often sitting in her wheelchair,
slumped over to the side. That's how her granddaughter found
her that morning. Lizzy was dozing with small rivulets of tears

streaking her tan cheeks.

So that day she was back in her place at the head of the painted kitchen table. Only this time there was no laughter, no loud flow of energy-filled love. The house was filled with people as usual, grandchildren, great-grandchildren, and even a new great-great-grandson who stared quizzically up at this wizened figure on wheels.

The room had been newly decorated the past spring, for Easter. The sheet rock ceiling was painted white, its untaped nail heads visible, pressing up the enamel paint like rows of string beans in a garden just beginning to push their heads through the warming soil. The walls had been papered, without the care to match the small flowered pattern. So while freshened and made bright with the new paint and paper, the room still gave a casual, comfortable air, a familiar feeling Lizzy must have been glad to come back to.

Lizzy's daughter, herself becoming grey and lined, kept conspicuously busy at the sink by the far wall. Knowing children entered the house and exited, careful not to slam the door, quiet and hushed with her presence. Lizzy was hungry and was pleased to smell the boiled dinner simmering on the electric stove. A large kettle of potatoes, cabbages, rutabagas, and carrots, flavored by a small piece of fat side-pork—a family favorite—was cooking. It was seasoned with salt and pepper.

In that house, it seemed, people lived in the kitchen. Only three other rooms existed: a front room for the television, hide-a-bed davenport, and vinyl recliner; the bathroom small enough for only one person at a time, and a single large upstairs bedroom with five beds ringing the walls. The small, wooden house was old, going back to the 1880's, when logging first came to the reserve.

When the boiled dinner was served someone gave a short prayer. Then one of the women cut the vegetables on Lizzy's plate into smaller pieces. Silently the family began to eat. Lizzy, her eyesight failing, probed for her food with her fork, like an arm searching for a light switch in a darkened room. Taking a piece of food and placing it carefully into her mouth, she would close her eyes and slowly chew. As I sat at the table, eating and watching her, I thought of how good this food must have tasted to her, this meal cooked by her daughter, here in these familiar surroundings.

A ten-year-old great granddaughter sat at the other end of the table, out of the room's traffic, eating while she looked at her great-grandmother, watching her slow, deliberate moves. This youngster, normally so full of life, a year ago would have run up to Lizzy and thrown her arms around her. Now the black haired, dark girl was silent. Like the rest of us, she asked in hushed tones for food to be passed. She ate slowly and quietly, watching Lizzy but trying to appear not to be doing so.

The dinner went on with no loud, happy stories. I thought how Lizzy was unlike some other old people in the nursing home who would quiver and shake uncontrollably. Her arms were dark, thin, and branch-like, but they were still controlled by her. But the problem with her eyesight was troublesome. Later I was told how that day on the ride home from the nursing home, when the car's windshield was flecked by the sunlight and passing tree shadows, that she told her granddaughter the falling snow was beautiful.

After the meal's main course was completed the table was cleared. A few people began cleaning up the dishes at the sink while some children ran outside to play. The rest of us remained at the table, our chairs pushed back, one or two lighting cigarettes. Lizzy, now filled with the hot food, dozed now and again, only to awake with a small start as she raised her tired head to glance at us. We chatted about the good food, careful not to lose sight of the importance of Lizzy's presence. Normally we would have been treated to stories, but that day we had to accept the end of those times.

Lizzy had very dark brown skin. I marveled at its deep rich color, a brown like warm, flowing milk chocolate. It was a healthy color. A silent, proud color. I was certain she was getting darker these past few years, yet she was rarely out in the sun. I recalled that in one version of the Ojibwe origin legend, the first people, the Anishinaabeg, were covered with a glistening, white enamel hardness that gave them immortality, and how the trickster, Wenebozo, as his solution to the problem of overpopulation, had removed it, making them susceptible to death. I felt that perhaps in her last days on earth this 91 year-old woman was expressing her Ojibwe-ness. Her overlay of whiteness was cracking and pieces had fallen away to expose her true self: an *Ojibwekwe*, an Ojibwe woman.

When Lizzy's daughter cut the apple pies she had baked that morning and placed pieces before each of us, a granddaughter reminded Lizzy that it was time to take her medication. So the granddaughter removed the large tan purse from the back of Lizzy's chair and handed it to her. Lizzy fumbled to undo the clasp, then probing within the vinyl bag came up with a vial of white tablets. She handed it to the granddaughter and asked for a glass of water. The pills were taken, then the pie was slowly eaten.

Most of us adults knew what was in the purse. A granddaughter looked inside one day in the nursing home while Lizzy slept. She came back from the visit and over coffee told us as we sat quietly. Among the contents were a time-yellowed and finger-worn snapshot of her son who was killed in Korea. Along with it was the telegram announcing his death, its yellow paper folded over and over from the endless times she must have opened it and refolded it. The other items were a small religious card from the Society of St. Joseph the boy had carried in his wallet and the little faded, stapled booklet of airmail stamps she had sent him. These latter two items were among the few contents found in his wallet that was sent to her by the authorities. These were all the material remnants she had of the son. She kept them as best as she knew how, in her dark purse, in its enclosed, warm void. He was at least safe there.

With the eating of the dessert, Lizzy fell into a deep sleep. Finally, the granddaughter announced she would take Grandma back to the home. We rolled the chair out of the small house, and I recall how Lizzy woke as we pushed her to the waiting automobile. *"Megwitch,"* she said, as we all gave her our farewell hugs. "Thank you, thank you all," she ended. "Good-bye Gram," most of us said as we quickly embraced her as she sat in the car. Soon the door was carefully closed and the granddaughter took the car's wheel and backed from the yard.

Court was over, I thought to myself as I watched the car move along the blacktopped road to town. Lizzy Roy had held court and once again her message was loud and clear. As she had taught us how to live she was now teaching us how to die. We listened and learned.

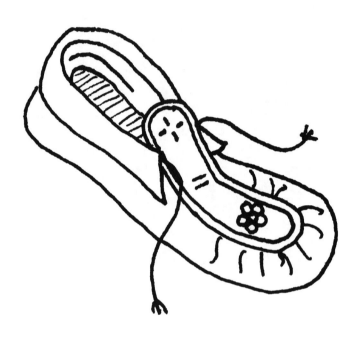

Pageantry

It lies on the north side of Red Cliff Creek, right at the bay. Eastward the land rises to a point out into Lake Superior before turning north to Frog Bay, with thirty to forty-foot high rocky cliffs, but moving west along the creek it comes back down to lowland. Probably in the distant past this was regularly inundated with spring runoff. Today this flat low grassy area is called the Pageant Grounds. This label is slipping away with the elders who were alive during World War I and the several years following. Now, younger generations know little about it, if anything. The last pageant was held over eighty years ago. Now, a scattering of young, seven foot white pines and a rush of alderbrush are starting to reclaim it.

Several years ago, Dianne DeFoe, a tribal member, wrote a paper on it for an undergraduate class. Sharing this with me, she pointed out the copies of old newspaper photos of shirtless men in feather headdresses on horseback, of the Model T Ford Roadsters parked at the group's periphery, and of White women in linen dresses and wide-brimmed hats.

In the 1920's enterprising railroad promoters advertised the Indian Pageant held there. Coal burning trains from Chicago and Milwaukee ran to Bayfield, bringing city folk to the north for a festive weekend. They were lodged in the small town's inns and driven the final five miles out from town to the reservation. Concessionaires hawked foods and drink of the day to the clean-clothed tourists.

The *Bayfield Press* of Aug. 13, 1925, told of the excitement
of the affair:

"The Pageant production this year is really a remarkable show,
with its intensive action as demonstrated in Indian battles and
early Indian life, and the manner in which the Indian perform-
ers, as well as the white actors, have entered into the spirit of the
production, denotes an intense interest."

I had never been on the old Pageant Grounds until an afternoon in October 1999. A brother-in-law and I had driven out
to walk over some old reservation land just north of the grounds
that was recently purchased from a downstate paper company
after years of being in non-tribal hands. Pleased with the acqui-
sition, we were quietly uplifted, hopeful that this parcel would
be the start of more to return.

When finished with our walk, we stepped back into my Jeep
and I headed down the forest trail out to the main blacktopped
road. Then, inexplicably, coming upon the smaller track leading down to Red Cliff Creek, without forethought, I turned
onto it. Perhaps buoyed by the supporting presence of my
brother-in-law, who surprisingly, had never been on the Pageant Grounds either, I said, "Let's do some exploring."

It was Apple Fest Weekend. The small town of Bayfield, five
miles to the south, and recently acclaimed by a Chicago newspaper writer to be the best vacation destination in the Midwest,
was bulging with weekend visitors. The festival was the culmi-
nation of a series of events running through the tourist season.
Traffic had flowed to town through the reservation Friday afternoon and again Saturday morning. On such weekends, my
brother-in-law and I enjoyed turning our backs on the crowds,
preferring the woods instead.

The Bayfield Peninsula has a history of hosting ceremonial
celebrations. Protestant missionary Sherman Hall, when sta-
tioned on Madeline Island, wrote how he was sometimes unable to minister to his tribal minions because they would disappear. Whether to get distant from him, or for other reasons,

they often left for the mainland, three miles away. He told in his diary of March 6, 1832, how at such a time, he took a boat to the mainland and found them, as he put it, "preparing for one of their heathenish dances." The Smithsonian ethno-musicologist Thomas Vennum, Jr., who writes about these things, suggests they were preparing for a Midewiwin ceremony and that they were on the shoreline near present day Red Cliff.

Another shoreline event, held even earlier—in 1808— and witnessed by historian Benjamin Foster, was held in an Ojibwe village, again very probably in or near Red Cliff. This was a gathering led by representatives of Tenskwatawa, the Shawnee Prophet. Tenskwatawa's brother was Temcumseh. This Shawnee twosome worked in tandem in the very early 1800's to unite the disparate tribal nations into a single force to repel the advance of the whites.

At this "celebration" the Ojibwe were told to discard their personal ritual possessions and to extinguish all fires. They must have responded in some numbers because Foster reports seeing medicine bundles of a thousand men washing up onto the Lake Superior shore. New fires were to be ignited the old way, with sticks, and the people were never to let them go out.

And the archives tell us more about this important shoreline. This time the event apparently occurred a bit more distant, but it surely involved Ojibwe with Red Cliff connections. Benjamin Armstrong, the chronicler of Ojibwe history in the Apostle Island Region and the interpreter who travelled with Buffalo to Washington, D.C. in 1852, wrote of a contingent of Ghost Dancers from the Great Plains who came to Chequamegon Bay. Armstrong says it was probably in 1887, and that they were "twenty miles west of Ashland, where the Lac Courte Orielles Trail and the White River meet."

He claims that "considerable excitement was caused in and around Ashland, Wisconsin, over a report in circulation that Indians were dancing and having pow wows further west and were working their way toward the reservations in this part of the country." Armstrong says that "There were between sixty

and seventy in the party which consisted of a young Sioux girl
and her interpreter, the balance being made up of Chippewas
from this immediate vicinity." He claims to have been an ob-
server at one of their "dances," and that the girl and her group
"remained here among the Chippewas some days" before heading west to Crow country.

The Ghost Dance, the Shawnee Prophet and the Midewiwin,
unlike the Bayfield Apple Festival, all addressed rebirth and renewal in serious religious ways. The Midewiwin always has,
and still does.

I kept the dark green Jeep moving along the narrow track.
We were in deep woods, and in a time of bright color and strong
aroma. This was fall. Leaves were detaching and floating to the
earth. Some already turning brown, many insect-holed, they
told of the season. The hardwoods were yellow, orange, and
red. The deep green conifers were just as stolid in holding their
finery.

Our windows were down. We breathed in the perfume. This
woods had not been logged for some time, the trees quite large,
unlike much of the reservation. We passed white cedars two
feet and more in diameter at the base. Cedars this large are very
rare here.

Then came the release of moving from thick wood to the
clearing. *Gichigami* lay before us. At the edge of the shore,
where the flat green ground gave itself over to the trees again,
were five swans lazily paddling on the lake. At first neither of us
mentioned them, but I stopped the truck and we watched for
several moments. Then, I said, "Tundra swans. Or do you think
they're trumpeters?" Embarrassed that we were not sure, finally
we agreed that they were the much more rare trumpeters —
"had to be." We both knew that we *wanted* them to be trumpeters. Close together, the large sunburnt-ivory-colored birds moved
as a unit, their long, sleek necks slowly swaying as they drifted
in a small circle.

I stopped the engine and we stepped down onto the earth.

We gently pushed our doors shut until they caught. Then we stepped out on to the green plane. We each went our own way for several minutes, very slowly walking over the grass. This was an old place, but new to both of us.

"This is where they danced! Right here! This is it! The drum ring was there, over there in the middle. This has to be it. This is the place," a pause, then "Jesus Christ!"

The brother-in-law, now 53, after high school, college, the Army service in Korea,—after this and more—was dancing. His blue and white checkered flannel shirt strugged to cover early signs of a middle-aged paunch. His long, thick, single black braid hanging down his back, moved from side to side, slowly, with the fluidity of the long-necked swans.

He danced, lifting one leg, then placing it carefully back onto the bent October grasses. Then the other as he leaned forward at the waist. His arms, bent upward at the elbow, held invisible dancing sticks. Mystic power wands.

Standing back to watch, to leave him be, not to interfere, I marvelled at his coordination, his easy movement. He was no longer with me, gone to dance with the others, eighty years ago. Was he the first to dance here in eighty years? Yes, I concluded, whether true or not. Let him have that joy.

Minutes later we left the low clearing to climb the gentle rise leading up to the heavy timber. There near the top, through a copse of seven-foot soft-needled white pines, was another clearing, smaller than the first.

"This is the parking lot, the camping place. Here," he waved an arm out to the opening and its hill beyond, "was where the families camped, slept, cooked." He raised his nose and with closed eyes breathed inward. "Wood smoke. Fires. Imagine."

We walked through the trees, picking up a faint track that eventually led to a small weathered wood-frame house. Single storied, its walls crumbling in places, its moss-heavy wooden shingled roof open on one side. Rain and snow work quickly.

A 1912 map of the reservation, in my possession, shows three small black square symbols in this exact spot. There were houses here back then. Was this one of them? My mother-in-law, born in 1920, recalls that a Peterson Family used to have a house here. The map also shows that the Indian Agency was located here, on this high ground. And it tells that a sawmill was nearby, toward the lake. A busy area in the late 1800's and early 1900's, this was the center of the reservation. Surely, I thought, people are buried in this ground, on this point. Mike Newago, an elder today, born in 1918, says this about the Pageant Grounds: *"That is where people used to come when they came to Red Cliff. That is the place."*

Among the several definitions my dictionary offers for the word pageant are *1) a specious display; unsubstantial pomp, and 2) a type of community drama based on local history, given by local actors, out of doors.* The historical fact that Ojibwe Indians of Lake Superior were not horseback people did not deter the promoters of the 1925 Red Cliff Indian Pageant from including bareback-riding Indians in the cast. It seems city people wanted to see real Indians ride horses beside Lake Superior. Why should the Roaring 20's have been a time that cared for historical accuracy? Apparently, in those years right after World War I, Indians and horses went together, no matter what tribe, no matter what place. People were willing to pay money to watch the spectacle, accurate or not.

The "community drama" I witnessed as my brother-in-law danced on the Old Red Cliff Pageant Grounds in October 1999, was "based on local history, was given by a local actor, and was out of doors." He "carried on the tradition" of dancing at Red Cliff Creek, beside Lake Superior. As he danced he was with those who did so in the past. He heard and felt the drumbeat. He smelled the wood smoke of the old fires. The missionary Sherman Hall might have called his dance "heathenish" and the 1925 tourists might have missed the horses, but his dance pleased me. It was, in fact, spectacular.

After exploring the tumble-down house we found a second. It did not have long before it, too, would fall. Filled now, we stood on the wooded ridge above the dancing ground before slowly walking back down to the Jeep. We gazed across the creek to its south shore. There we saw the jumble of buildings that has risen on that spot over the past many years. In the hands of non-tribal members, the area is highlighted by a small marina, frequented largely by moneyed people from Minneapolis and St. Paul.

"How long before all that jumps the creek?" I asked.

There was a long space of silence, then my brother-in-law quietly uttered, "Damn, God Damn."

We walked back to the Jeep and continued along the track as it looped up the ridge and into the woods. We kept going, not knowing when or where it would end. We expected to meet a dead-end soon, having to turn around and retrace out tracks. But, unexpectedly, the track led us on and finally we came to the original trail, the one we used when first driving into the woods to examine the newly-purchased land. It was then that we realized we had made a circle.

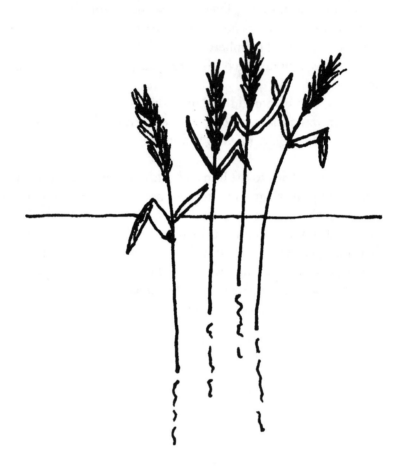

Repatriation

*Ojibway people continue to associate wild
rice with sacred matters.*
— Thomas Vennum, Jr., 1988

Last summer the cabin log had an entry by a young couple,
friends of our youngest son. It told of their pleasures in
being able to use the cabin for a weekend. City dwellers,
they both needed a hit of Nature, of solitude. They enjoyed not
having electric lights, running water, or hearing the muffled roar
of traffic. The outhouse suited them just fine.

The two page entry went on with gratitude and told of deer
sighted at dawn and of eagles working the creek. Then, at the
end, almost as an afterthought, it told of two men "from the
tribe" who appeared at the cabin on Saturday afternoon and
used our canoe to sow the lagoon with wild rice.

And it took. In fall it filled the channel, rising four to five
feet above the water, its heavy heads hanging down, glistening
in the morning sun. *Manoomin.* Wild rice. Ojibwe soul food.

We were thrilled. In the nearly forty years I have been coming to Red Cliff I had never found wild rice in any of its waters.
It was a crop that grew a bit further to the south. The famous
Kakagon Sloughs on the Bad River Reservation east of Ashland
is known for its rice, some Red Cliff people allowed to harvest it
at times. No one at Red Cliff recalls having it on their reservation.

The literature is also silent on rice at Red Cliff. While the other Wisconsin Ojibwe communities—Bad River, Lac Courte Orielles, Lac du Flambeau, Sokaogon, and St. Croix—have it, none is written about at Red Cliff. Surely the large bay and slough at Sand River is a good spot for rice. Raspberry River's shallow stretches likewise. Was it ever there?

Thomas Vennum, of the Smithsonian Institution, tells me he found no mention of wild rice at Red Cliff when he did the research for his book on rice and the Ojibwe. However, he suggests it might have been there in the distant past. The level of Lake Superior has fluctuated, and this could have caused its loss. But shouldn't this have been a problem at the Kakagon Sloughs as well?

So the wild rice crop at Red Cliff in 1999 seemed to be the first such crop for over one hundred years. I interviewed Mary and Joe Roy in the 1960's at Red Cliff, and they had never known the grain to be growing in any of their waters. They were both born in the nineteenth century. If we use the journals of missionary Sherman Hall, who was on Madeline Island in the 1830's, we might agree that the absence of rice at Red Cliff probably goes back at least to that time. Hall complains that the Ojibwe would regularly leave the island to hunt and make sugar, but he says nothing about them going to the Red Cliff shoreline for a fall rice harvest.

Whether or not the plant was ever growing at Red Cliff is unclear, but it is certain that it is there now. Larry Deragon, one of the men who sowed Frog Creek Slough, told me "We will keep sowing each year until we get a good catch." There is strong determination to succeed. Although the people may not have had their own rice fields in the early years, they want them now. In the past, as today, they were able to harvest rice in some inland lakes as guests of other Ojibwe communities. Most often, however, they acquired the grain by trading for it, or purchasing it from tribesmen on other reserves.

Sometimes tribal members ventured out of what was then deemed "Indian Country" to harvest the grain. In an interview in the 1970's Red Cliff's Johnny Buffalo told me how when he was a youth he and his father would harvest the grain in Minnesota waters. He said:

"My dad had an old Ford truck, one of those with the open back like a pickup truck. One year we drove way over there— it was on a lake southwest of Duluth. We set up our tent. We were getting a lot but on the second day when we were out on the water we saw this black smoke coming from the shore. It was our truck. Those white guys had set it afire. They didn't want us Indians to take their rice. We had to hitchhike home."

Johnny was born in 1905, and he thought he was about ten or twelve years old when this happened. So it might have been in World War I times. (In a number of ways those were not always good days for the Ojibwe—or for other people of color. The infamous Duluth, Minnesota, lynchings occurred in the 1920's.) When I asked what ever came of the truck incident he said, "Nothing did. What could we do?" he replied. When I think of the Red Cliff people who harvest rice today in off-reservation ceded lands I am reminded how important the old treaties really are.

These days wild rice is an important menu item at Red Cliff. I have always known it to be present at the big gatherings. But, usually it is said to be "Odanah rice"—coming from Bad River. Odanah, the village at Bad River (and the word for town in the Ojibwe language), has many people who harvest it. It provides food, a source of cash, and serves as valued gifts. Feasts have wild rice. Along with venison, lake trout, whitefish, and maple sugar (or syrup), this "good grain" forms the list of traditional foods generally found in Wisconsin's Ojibwe communities today. At least these are the current favorites.

In days past other menu items were found. *Waabooz* (rabbit), fiddleheads (the coiled tops of young ferns), *bine* (pronounced partridge by many Red Cliff people), *mizay* (a form of catfish), *adikameg* (whitefish throats that take the shape of a small clay pipe when boiled), fried *waakisan* (eggs of numerous varieties of fish) — all these have been served at tables I have been at. And stories are told of other foods, which I have not been fortunate enough to have eaten, but which in some cases still show up on a table now and then. These are not just foods of the past. *Gaag* (porcupine) and *makwa* (black bear) come to mind.

In the early 1800's, with the coming of the *Chi-mookomaan* (the white man), the Ojibwe menu changed. Pork became a favorite. If no ham, ribs, loins, or roasts were available, many households were able to get a small chunk of salt pork to give other dishes the valued pork taste. This continues today. I have sat down to what was called a roast beef dinner only to find that a chunk of pork was roasted along with the beef, in the same pan. It seems pork was a flavoring of choice. A family story tells how a white man from Bayfield who married into a Red Cliff family once remarked that, "A Red Cliff woman can't cook without salt, pepper, and pork."

The nutty, grassy flavor of wild rice along with its chewy, almost crunchy texture, has been a favorite of mine for years. When I first came to the reservation, wild rice was usually served with cream of mushroom soup. Not as two separate menu items, they were typically mixed together into a casserole, similar to those Garrison Keillor claims are served in Lake Wobegon.

Today at Red Cliff, it is still occasionally served this way. But I feel that increasingly it is being served without the soup. This pleases me. Wild rice is starting to stand alone, without the help of flavoring. More and more, when at a Red Cliff feast, I am able to take large portions of boiled wild rice—without anything added, except perhaps a dash of salt and pepper that the cook might have felt, "it just needed." *Manoomin* is starting to be accepted as it once was, for itself. I have been told this is "the old way." It certainly is the way to receive the grain's traditional flavor and essence.

As in the past, wild rice is a great connector at Red Cliff. I have seen it appear at Christmas time, a pound or so, in a small plastic sack tied with a short red ribbon. While the house might be filled with the chatter of a family gathering, an uncle will step into another room and reappear with such a small sack. He hands it to a niece who lives in a distant state but brings her family home each Christmas. She accepts the gift, might say very little, or nothing at all, but might give him a quick hug. This is classic Ojibwe gift-giving. There is no need for words at such a time. The niece will take it with her on the plane. She will serve it at those special times and will be mystically transported to the reservation when she does. Her young children will learn the importance of *manoomin*, of being Ojibwe.

Wild rice is a symbol of Ojibwe identity. And as such it is being given more and more respect at Red Cliff. Any meals are usually quiet, almost contemplative affairs on the reservation, but it seems to me that this is especially true in the handling, preparation, serving, and eating of wild rice. Some Ojibwe say this appreciative silence should be observed when out in the rice fields during the harvest. It seems in such times the only noises heard should be those made as the boat is poled through the water along with the gentle rhythmic sounds as the ripe grain is "knocked" into the boat.

Traditionally all food is viewed as gifts from the *manidoog*. The times of eating, then, are times of a coming together of the people and these spirits. Such an interaction is no little matter. And at some time wild rice and other valued objects pass back to the spirits. Sometimes a plate of food is prepared and quietly placed outdoors, at the base of a tree perhaps, for the *manidoog*. Other times offering bundles, that can include wild rice, are prepared and placed in or on the water, or in other significant places. This reciprocity is a given in Ojibwe culture.

It is this sanctity, this deep importance of wild rice, that might cause some Ojibwe to say that humans should never try to plant the grain. Herein lies the source of the deeply felt antagonism sometimes shown toward cultivated paddy rice. It is also leveled at The University of Minnesota's research efforts in trying to improve the artificial growing of the grain. Traditionalists suggest that the planting of wild rice is an instance of interfer-

ence with the *manidoo* world. Such aggressive actions toward
the grain is a "forcing" of the human and *manidoo* relationship.
So the planting of rice at Red Cliff in 1999 probably is viewed
by some Ojibwe in this negative way. Like my fascination with
wild flowers, this planting could be said to be overdoing it, going too far. The spirits cannot be forced to act. In Ojibwe
religious belief they are in control of things. Humans should be
accepting, and should abide by the rules. They should live right
and wait.

Barry Lopez speaks of "the distance of reason." Our Western
rationalization, our penchant to search, to question, is a part of
our world view that we hold dear. This is a direct legacy of what
the Europeans call "The Enlightenment." But in this rush to
reason we find dissenters. Traditionalists worldwide hesitate at
times with our desire to know. At these times they shift from
knowing through science to a knowing through belief.

The coming of wild rice to Red Cliff in 1999 is not unlike
the coming of other things. The traditional pow wow held in
early July for the past several years is the return of something
very old. The purification lodges have also returned, or perhaps
if it is felt they never left, have more recently come out in the
open. Clothing and hairstyle changes have been made in the
last thirty to forty years. And there are numerous other changes,
sometimes not readily visible to the outside eye.

Red Cliff's decision to plant the rice is part of a concerted
effort to maintain an old relationship with the land. Perhaps it
is felt that rice belongs in the reservation's sloughs and shallow
water regions. Even if it never grew along this Lake Superior
shoreline, it certainly seems to have a good fit. It feels like rice
belongs on this shoreline, in this community. Wild rice is not
intrusive.

In his recent book on traditional Ojibwe culture, *(We Have
A Right To Exist)*, the Red Lake, Minnesota, writer, Wubekeniew,
writes about *permaculture*. He feels the Ojibwe practice this

when they utilize the foods of the forest, waters, air, and clearings. By seasonally returning to places where food is found, and by not changing these places, with minimal intrusion, the tribal people maintain a more or less permanent food source. But there is more, for Wubekeniew insists this is a much more sane human adaptation than found in present day post-industrial capitalistic societies. Ecologically, permaculture is much more sound.

Perhaps *manoomin* is like others who are returning to the Northland. Timber wolves, cougars, fishers and pine martens are all said to be coming back to the Lake Superior woods. Some early religious items are very quietly finding their way back. Attempts are being made to help sweetgrass propagate and thrive. And some Ojibwe reservations, as at Bad River and Lac Courte Orielles, have recently undertaken serious initiatives to increase the use of Ojibwemowin, the Ojibwe language. This is being done with a deep, quiet passion. Although its speakers are few, Red Cliff has not lost the old language. Today, lengthy discourses in Ojibwemowin are starting to be heard at important social gatherings at Red Cliff. Tribal members like Mark Gokee, Delores Bainbridge and others work to bring this about. Such recoveries and returns of custom are quiet. This is the traditional way. And it all takes time. There is little, if any, hoopla.

One day two men walked down the path to Frog Creek. They carried a sack of wild rice. They borrowed a canoe and scattered the grain onto the water. There was no fanfare, no loud crowd. No ribbons were cut. Like the pine marten, they came quietly into the woods. Tobacco was put down. The task accomplished.

And who knows if the rice will reseed itself and come back next year? Even with the planned successive plantings it might fail. But one pleasant event has already occurred because of the rice's catch at Frog Creek. Last fall, for the first time in over twenty years, a small flock of *nikag* (Canada geese) spent several weeks in the area, feeding on the grain. It was a pleasure to have them, to see them in the lagoon in front of the cabin, stretching their necks to reach the food.

In 1978 the United States Congress passed the Indian Graves
and Repatriation Bill. It decreed that human remains and certain cultural items from native communities now held by colleges, universities, and museums must be returned, when possible, to their respective tribes. Recently the Omaha people of
Nebraska saw the Harvard Peabody Museum return the tribe's
sacred pole. Many other instances of returns have taken place.
So far nothing has been officially returned to Red Cliff.

A few years ago my wife and I attended an anthropological
conference in Cleveland, Ohio. We were pleasantly startled to
come upon a large glass case holding a display of Great Lakes
tribal paraphernalia. In its center was a large and quietly striking *wiigwaasi-makak*. The birch bark container stood approximately three feet tall, with a diameter of about 20 inches. Such
wiigwaasi-makakoon rarely come that large. Its identifying tag
said it was from Red Cliff, Wisconsin, and had been collected
in the 1920's. Its craftsperson is now gone. We stood before
this magnificent object and wondered what other things from
Red Cliff might have found their way to museums.

At Red Cliff the land is still there. In some places it is owned
by others. It is marked with a highway and other roads. It has
been logged again and again. Its waters have been fished, over-
fished, invaded by the sea lamprey and the ruffe, and probably
will see the coming of other saltwater invaders. But white pine
seedlings are found. In the spring the gentle doe still drops her
spotted fawn. The language is still heard. And now hopefully,
manoomin will be here, too.

Red Clay

—the human heart and the land have been
brought together so regularly in human history.
— Barry Lopez, 1989

There is a harshness to the Lake Superior shoreline. This is clearly seen on the rugged north shore of Minnesota and up into Ontario, where black rock outcroppings stand exposed to the poundings of the big lake. Photographers, painters, poets, and postcard makers are drawn to the north shore again and again. They seem fascinated by its barren strength. They come to witness a battle between rock and water.

On the north shore, both land and lake appear bigger than life, each opposed to the other yet neither giving way. In their toughness they become like each other. And one is as unassailably beautiful as the other. This joining of giants is captured by Gwekigenahgahboo (George Morrison), the celebrated Ojibwe artist from Grand Portage, Minnesota. After leaving his community as a young man and making his way in the "bigger" world of Minneapolis, New York City, and the European meccas of the art scene, he came home to paint and sculpt this meeting of land and water—only Morrison, with his Ojibwe grasp of things, included another giant: the sky.

Morrison's simple and powerful images of the eastern horizon—often nothing more than a horizontal line on canvas or wood—are enough.

But this is the north shore. To a Minnesotan it seems obvious. It is well known as a weekend and vacation destination, especially for those tired Twin City dwellers.

We do not hear about the big lake's south shore in the same way. Wisconsin's (and Michigan's) south shore of Lake Superior is celebrated differently. With few exceptions, this shoreline has another character, perhaps a gentler one. One might conclude that here the winds off the lake are calmer, the stern rock outcroppings more receptive. And perhaps this would be the truth, or at least it is an image that promoters of tourism on the south shore try to depict.

Certainly, a calm serenity can be found along Lake Superior's south shore. But just as certain are the whipping November winds that come into its bays and batter its projecting headlands. On the south shore, the Apostle Islands buffet the Red Cliff shoreline from some of this. Devil's Island, especially with its famed sea caves, shows centuries of battle with strong waves.

In obvious ways the Bayfield Peninsula is like Minnesota's north shore. Both stand high at times, against the lake. But unlike the north shore, this southern shore is colored a deep red. Hence, the European name for the community the Ojibwe call Passibikaning. Red Cliff. The legends tell of the color coming from Wenabozho's blood. Early on, these cliffs with their red sandstone outcroppings were well known as markers for people on the lake. Familiar names in Ojibwe literature, like Schoolcraft, Nicolet, Radisson and Grossiellers, wrote about them.

This southern shoreline has its own harshness. At times of storms, the big lake can be merciless in its pounding of this land. In these storms, rock outcroppings along the beach stand as rows of armored lance-bearing soldiers facing the adversary. But it is not just in hard times that the land's fierceness is visible. All year long, in the quiet times as in the loud, the land's serious presence can be felt. It can be unforgiving in any season. Whether its the needled mosquitos of June, those damnedably persistent biting black flies that come in July, the few days of stifling humid air in early August, or winter's seriously biting cold, the land always tells you it is there.

Years ago, after spending enough time in the region to slow down and pay attention, I began to study the land. It was then, at Red Cliff, that I saw its unrelenting toughness. There was little forgiveness in it. Even in the towns of Cornucopia, Bayfield, Washburn and Ashland, that, as I was told "were more settled than the reservation," this harshness of the terrain was obvious. This was glacial country, formed out of the unstopablility of huge mountains of ice. Evidence of geological upthrusts, shifts, fissures and the heavy scraping of rock against rock seemed everywhere. The soil itself, when I took it into my hand, with its rough-edged pebbles, its sharp texture, felt uncomfortable, its resistance clearly evident. When walking along Bayfield's main street I saw how the buildings had to struggle to gain purchase with this land. Hillside houses held even more tightly to the earth, lest they slip down to the lake.

And the lake, with a fit of imagination on my part, was like a resting volcano. In geological time it had only recently been formed out of melting ice, but the cold could come again and the lake could climb out of its depths, to once again move over the land. Frozen, the lake would be like an Ojibwe cannibal ice-monster, *wiindigoo,* consuming all in its path.

I was told about Bayfield's flood of 1942, when the town's cemetery further up on the hillside, gave way, the caskets of its dead washing down into town. It was like a belching up, a refusal of the land to take anymore of the treatment humans had been subjecting it to. It was an owl's call: an omen. Surely, I concluded, this northern land is something to be dealt with.

I was familiar with the rolling hills of central and southern Wisconsin. In those places the earth was softer, more giving, surely more gentle in how it received us. There was a calmness over this land. Contrariwise, in the far north, perhaps I was unknowingly uneasy with the might of Lake Superior that was always in the background, even on the calmest of summer days. When first coming to this north land, I looked to see what the people did here—how they made their living. I felt it was not a good place for farming. It was the *north land,* a place with other possibilities. Yet on my first trip up I immediately saw farms, and some seemed to be successful enough. But agriculture that far north was pushing things. In Wisconsin, the longer growing season and the better soil are further south. When I mentioned this to someone I was usually told of the familiar "lake effect." Lake Superior's large water mass was said to affect weather patterns nearby. The fruit growers of Bayfield take advantage of this and have success. Since those early times, I have concluded that the "effects" of Lake Superior can play themselves out in interesting ways.

During the second half of the nineteenth century at Red Cliff, missionaries and government agents made gestures to turn the Ojibwe into farmers. With the passage of the Dawes Allotment Act in 1887, these gestures were given official sanction. The annual reports of agents on the reservation in those years tell us exactly how many acres of woods were cleared, how many rods of fence were strung, how many bushels of potatoes were grown. But in time the land won out. The Jeffersonian ideal of the countryman in his fields did not seem to work in the north woods. Tales of the northern Wisconsin "cutover" come to mind, with their images of European immigrants attempting to break the stump-laden land only to have the land break them.

So I was sure farming was not a reasonable possibility. And yet, today the well trimmed farmstead of the State of Wisconsin's Agricultural Extension Service continues to sit, as a showpiece, out along Highway 2, west of Ashland. Poised as an outpost on a frontier, its denial is striking. We are still trying to break this northern land.

Many times, with a shovel in hand, I have had to confront this land. In the earliest days, whenever I had to work with it I cursed it. On much of the reservation it comes in the form of red clay. At breakup time each March and April the driveways are rut-filled and your boots become heavy and large as clown feet. Then, in July and August when we yearn for a cloudy sky and the moisture it can bring, it can be as intractable as hardened cement. At such times earthworms are at a premium. You usually can find a few along creek bottoms, but if you dig out behind the house you won't get many. You won't dig long back there either, because you'll have to work too hard.

Still, it's strange. Even in the times of heat the garden hangs on, especially if the spring was wet. Tomatoes must send their roots down deep for they are known to thrive in the clay. Today's gardens can be very successful, but I am told it is nothing compared to what it used to be. People say that before World War II, "everyone" on The Rez had gardens. Substantiated by the old writings going back into the 1800's, these were usually along creek beds where thin layers of dark loam covered the deeper clay.

Such family gardens were relied on for food, the people preserving it for winter. Seeds were ordered ahead of time for starting indoors and sometimes the dark humus of nearby woods was gathered and spread over garden plots. A favorite way to fertilize back then was to set a wooden barrel beside the creek, put a few forkfuls of cow manure into it and then fill it full of water. The next day the tea was poured onto the garden.

At Red Cliff, I have seen vegetables growing in red clay in ways I thought impossible. Beets stood in rows, pushing the hardened chunks of earth away. Tomatoes stood green and hearty, apparently very pleased with the ground. This was always quite interesting for me. I was raised on the heavy dark loam of central and southern Wisconsin, so Lake Superior's red clay seemed an oddity. In my early years at Red Cliff it seemed useless and troublesome—hard in summer and a slippery, sticky mess in spring and fall. I considered it a burden the Ojibwe had to live with, a price to pay for being in the otherwise wonderful northern forest beside the big lake. To me it must have been a deal cut with the Big Gambler, even a trick *Wenabozo* played on the *Anishinaabeg*.

This lament was with me a number of years ago when I labored to dig holes for foundation posts for our Frog Creek cabin. That incident was one of my first extended efforts to deal with the toughness of the clay. It was in late August when I spent several days camped at the wooded site beside the creek. I dug the holes by hand, fourteen of them, with a regular hand shovel. Each was at least five feet deep and it was red clay all the way down. Fourteen five-foot holes with a diameter of about sixteen inches.

It was hot and there were mosquitoes. At sundown after a meal of warmed beans, sausage, and smoked Earl Grey tea, I'd crawl into my blue pup tent, exhausted. The fire crackled an hour or two into the settling darkness, and as owls started their nightly choruses, I'd quickly fall to sleep cursing the clay. I recall dreams of tractors with shiny hydraulic augers that smoothly spiraled their way down through the ground, but I'd wake to blistered hands, aching muscles and a shovel handle darkened from salty sweat. When the holes were dug and the cedar posts set and tamped, I broke camp and walked the mile to the blacktop road with feelings of real accomplishment.

But putting a shovel to the earth in a search for fishing worms, for tilling a garden, and for setting foundation posts of a cabin the woods is joyful digging. Such labor is laden with warm expectations. The pleasures of going fishing, of enjoying fresh homegrown vegetables, and the welcome anticipation of cabin things like fireplaces, sweet wood smoke and warm cozy sunsets through the trees can make the arduous task of digging in red clay almost worthwhile.

In the mid-1970's, I was doing another kind of digging. It demanded I go deeper than I have ever gone. An elder had died and a grave had to be dug. It was mid-November and frost was in the ground. It would be difficult work. In those years, as generally continues today, graves were dug by hand.

So, on a Saturday morning I hurried up to the cemetery that rests on the rise across the ravine just north of the white clapboard church. The lake lies about one hundred yards to the east and can be seen through the aspens, and Chicago Creek flows quickly but silently through the spruce and oak woods just to the north. A few large hemlock trees border the burial ground on that side, their tiny brown cones covering the earth beneath them. It was a cold, overcast day and occasionally some rain fell, rain that wanted to be ice.

In the distance I saw a group of men busy at the grave site. As I walked across the ravine's path and climbed the rise, their low conversation became audible. Sporadic laughter drifted down the hill through the cold wind. They had broken through the frost and were about a foot and a half down. The grave was carefully placed between two others, and a pile of red clay rose to the north of the opening, slowly growing larger, spilling out over one of them. I was ready to sweat and to confront the demon red clay once again.

The digging was being overseen by a nephew of the deceased. Grey-haired, the nephew had been in the Ashland hospital recovering from back surgery when the death occurred. He insisted on being released early and taking charge of the digging. So there he sat, on a gravestone beside the opening, telling the younger men what needed to be done and how to do it. It was cold and his green work pants bulged over a suit of long underwear. The collar of his quilted blue jacket was turned up and the flaps of his cloth workman's cap tried to warm his ears. The younger men were not so protected. There were four of them, all grandsons of the deceased, and all were big-handed, big-shouldered, big-bellied men.

We took turns. A small ledge of short clay steps was left on the east side of the hole so we could easily enter and exit as the excavation proceeded. No large chunks of clay were tossed out of the opening, only small pieces, laboriously pried from the earth's red crust. This grave was being dug a little at a time.

On my second trip down, I felt the sweat forming on my arms, forehead, and shoulders. I used a flat, bladed long-handled ice chisel to slowly break away the small chunks and then tossed them up with a shovel. I worked steadily but slowly as the men above laughed and joked about how weak white men are. On my third trip down, I started to think of the graves just to my right and left. A casket lay on each side of me only two feet away through the earth walls. I knew both people lying there and I remembered them as they had been.

When I think of it now—when I reflect back on that morning—it seemed like I was visiting those two. It's like I was back in their kitchens, drinking coffee, eating sliced ring bologna on pieces of homemade bread, laughing with them. It's funny, maybe, but I felt no queasiness down in that grave, no fear. I never even thought about those two narrow walls crumbling and caskets sliding down onto me. Until very recently, few cement rough boxes were used here.

No one talked of death that morning. We chatted, laughed, joked. No one complained of the cold rain that fell on us now and then. An eagerness was evident, an eagerness for each to take his turn in the deepening grave. Bixie Cadotte joined us and soon Sheriff Bill arrived with his squad car, bringing coffee and bakery goods from town. He was the oldest grandson of the deceased and soon, uniform and all, was down in the hole, chipping away. Then, soft-spoken Bixie started spinning his yarns. Everyone knows Bixie. He worked for years in the plywood plant in town, and later was the driver for the company, driving that semi-trailer all over the Midwest. Bixie Cadotte is a respected man. His family name goes back to the eighteenth century in Lake Superior country, back to Jean Baptiste and Michael Cadotte, the French traders.

Bixie chipped away at the hard red clay. Between his shifts he told of other graves he dug. He told of the war and how he fought it. He told of people who lived in town during the war and how when he came home on furlough, he was surprised how some of the women were behaving while their men were away—far away in places like Sicily and Spain.

All of this went on at once. The coffee drinking, the doughnut eating, the chiseling away at the earth, the laughter, the joking—all of this going on in the cold November wind on that hill and all overseen by the elderly man seated on the head-stone.

When two or three feet of earth remained, another digger arrived, a young man, a great-grandson of the deceased. His red eyes and still flushed face told of a night in town. He had forced himself out of bed, certain not to miss his chance to help with the digging. We welcomed him with steaming coffee, a warm, sweet, heavily frosted cinnamon roll, and the heavy, long handled homemade ice chisel. He eagerly took his place in the rotation of diggers.

Soon a car stopped at the pathway and a woman hurried up the hill with another Thermos of coffee. She too was welcomed but she didn't stay. This was a man's place today.

Between my turns, I squatted by the old man and listened to his commands. He rose now and then to check the progress, to measure the hole's depth. We admonished him to stay seated, not to injure his back. He laughed at us. His tools were two green aspen poles, freshly from the nearby wood, bent and angling as aspens often are. In his hands and under his eyes these crude poles made the grave's walls straight, its corners perfectly placed. In those gnarled hands the homemade poles became straight as a surveyor's stadia rod and as precise as an expensive transit.

On my last trip into the now deep grave, I chiseled away the clay stairs. I removed little bits and slowly tossed them to the surface. It was during that work that I admitted my pleasure with the task. It occurred to me that I was working with red clay but I was relaxed, not all tight inside. During that cold November morning, I had crossed the barrier to acceptance. The four red walls that surrounded me offered warmth—a sanctuary from the cold air above. For the first time in over twenty years of confronting red clay, I wasn't fighting it.

When the stairs were removed and shoveled to the surface, I began to level the floor. Someone handed down a grub hoe and I started to peel a thin layer off the floor, working from east to west, but shouting from above interrupted me. It was our elderly overseer. I just wasn't doing it right. Finally, with the help of big hands thrust down, I was pulled from the hole. Quickly he took my place and in silence carefully removed the last layer, assuring the floor was level. He handed up the tools and we carefully reached down to help him climb out, contentment in his eyes. The grave was dug.

The next day, Sunday, the funeral took place. I had to stay with the funeral party but I wanted to stand back under the large hemlock trees with my digging friends from the day before. They stood quietly, watching and waiting for the ceremony to end so they could say their good-byes in their own ways, shovels in their hands.

The pile of red clay stood beside the open grave like an important member of the funeral party. There was no imitation green plastic grass to cover the bare earth. It was left exposed, visible, to be seen, and felt, by those who could see and feel it. As I stood in the crowd—no digging clothes today—I listened to the young white priest with cigarette-smoke colored fingers, who stood with his back to the mound of earth. He talked briefly, as he had inside the church, of the Holy Land. He talked of the savior and of olive trees. He talked of dry, sandy, rocky places, far away across the sea.

Despite the colorful beaded key holder that hung conspicuously from his waistline, he did not mention aspens, balsams, hemlocks, the big lake, or red clay. The people listened, but I noticed that many of them, especially the older, darker ones, stood with their shiny Sunday shoes on red clay and their eyes on the casket, the open grave, and the large red mound beside it.

Unlike the day before this was a bright sunny day. The sky was clear and a dark blue. The red of the earth and blue of the sky joined together on that hill that morning. Red and blue, I recalled, are the sacred colors of the ancient Ojibwe religion, the Midewiwin. I felt this, and when I looked at the men standing under the hemlocks, still in yesterday's clothes, I was sure they felt it too.

The Elder we buried that morning had lived her life in these woods. She was born in the 1800's and witnessed the shoreline before its destruction during the logging era. She knew its pleasures and certainties. Her stories, how it used to be, would live on to be told by the next person who became the teller of times of the past. Now, she was becoming in a final way, part of this *place*. Her final journal was beginning.

The several other times I have been at work in the Red Cliff cemetery also caused a degree of contemplation. Once, in the distant past, I used a camera rather than a shovel. I spent hours late on an unbelievable fall day frantically using the precious sunlight when it was precisely at the angle required for good photos. Some of the graves go back nearly a hundred years, their stones still legible. Some give the names in Ojibwemowin; the language. I was enthralled with all this history. A few weeks later I happily showed the photos—I had used colored slide film—at an evening family get-together. We gathered in one of the reservation's living rooms after a big meal. The earlier shots of family members brought the usual warm laughter, but when the first slide from the cemetery flooded onto the screen there was silence. After a few more cemetery shots I heard a masculine voice in the back of the room quietly utter, "What's the matter with that feller—taking pictures in the cemetery?"

Traditionally Ojibwe cemeteries are not places to spend much time. Even the spirits of the recently dead are to leave them quickly. Ideally cemeteries should be left alone, to be visited by the living only to bury someone, then to bring food for the deceased on the required number of days after the death.

Lawn mowers should not be heard in them, for if they are made too presentable, too trimmed and "beautiful," the spirits might spend too much time there, coming back regularly. When spirits come back too often it is said they are lonely. They are looking for companions to take back to the hereafter. For the living, this is to be avoided. So an untrimmed reservation cemetery, to me, is as it should be. It is where the Manidoo World reclaims what was really always its own.

The presence of elaborate stone grave markers in Ojibwe burial grounds demands thought. Twenty or more years ago, when on an automobile trip back to the Midwest from a conference in Seattle, my wife and a son drove up to Nespelem, Washington. We wanted to visit the grave of famed Nez Perce leader Chief Joseph. He died in 1904. We found it on a dry rise of land outside of the little reservation town. The good-sized cemetery, still in use, had no commercially made gravestones except for a tall marble column marking where Joseph was buried. It had been erected by the State of Washington.

In the years after his death, Joseph's fame spread. He became someone the larger national society could relate to. He became a hero for the United States and it seems that this "greater society" felt his grave needed to be marked in a manner fitting his historical stature. Today, you can usually find it marked on highway maps, especially those meant for the use of tourists.

Clearly, with the lone stone marker in that cemetery, and with its comparatively imposing presence (if my memory is correct, it was about five or six feet tall) Joseph's grave commanded attention. Whether correct or not, I concluded that unlike the Historical Society of the State of Washington, the rest of the Nez Perce people preferred to use simpler grave markers. They placed fist-sized cobbles, in the shape of an elongated circle, onto each grave.

Today at Red Cliff you see some newer graves being marked with what appear to be costly commercially made grave stones. Some of these newer stones are homemade, fashioned from poured concrete—shaped by hand. And many graves hold only a simple small wooden board cross, again homemade. From time to time some of these are painted white, but others are left to weather into a permanent grey. Some have names and dates painted onto them, in black, but for many these identfications are lacking.

The older part of the cemetery—some graves going back to the 1800's— lies closer to the lake. It holds early commercially made grave markers as well as several cast-iron crosses. Over the years several of these have taken a leaning, tilting stance. These elaborate stone markers and rusted old iron crosses are evidence of some affluence, during what is now called the Lumbering Era, when the huge white pines were being cut and a degree of money flowed into, and out of, the community. This portion of the cemetery is rarely visited anymore.

Using stone and steel was not the earliest Ojibwe way to mark a grave. I see a message here. Are these stones and steel crosses an imposition? Do they signal a "holding on" to passed loved ones that bespeaks of newer ways? Whatever the case, it is in the older part of the Red Cliff cemetery where the grasses go uncut. Here the aspens, balsams and other forest trees are moving in. The old large stone grave markers and their cast iron companions offer an interesting scene, standing side by side with the young trees as if they are genuine companions. Here the dead are merging with the land.

The Red Cliff shoreline has, for long, been a place for burying the dead. The act of burial consecrates a dwelling place. In this way a people claim a land as they settle onto it, indisputably establishing a location. With the burial of their dead they literally become part of the earth. A homeland is established.

Written records document the burial of an Ojibwe boy along this fingernail of land back in the 1830's, but surely burials go back much further than that. Practically no archeology has been done on Wisconsin's Bayfield Peninsula—except for some rather extensive work done on Madeline Island and a few more recent national park surveys—so we rely on oral traditon and early written documentation as evidence in a quest for the earliest human activity on this land. Where humans live is where they dispose of their dead. The records tell us Ojibwe people have been on this land for over three hundred years. Before them there were others. Humans have been on the North American continent for well over ten thousand years and recently this figure has been pushed back even earlier.

Reservation Elders tell of burial grounds on the lakeside of "The Big Hill" just south of the reserve towards Bayfield precisely where, in the early decades of the 1900's, a Chicago automobile dealer who did some Northern Wisconsin land speculating, attempted some farming. I suspect there are burials at Roy's Point, a place of much Ojibwe activity well up into the twentieth century but now overrun with vacation houses for the upscaled. While the waters at Roy's Point remain Red Cliff fishing grounds, its land has practically become off-limits to the reserve's people.

I have learned of at least five other burial sites at Red Cliff. Clearly, human burials are spread throughout all the tribe's lands, even out in the Sand River region at the far western end of the old reservation.

This is another reason why the entire shoreline is revered. Perhaps the act of burial domesticates this harsh land. Certainly, it is an act of acceptance that reinforces the notion of place. Through death, a peace is made. The people and the harsh shoreline with its tough, red clay receive each other in a final conciliatory embrace.

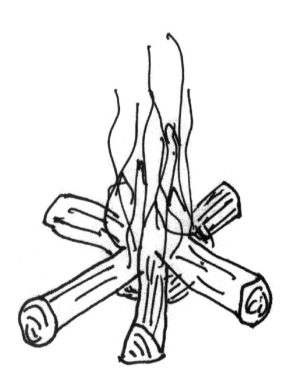

Pow wows

I am in the front yard of an uncle's small Red Cliff home. It stands on a rise overlooking Lake Superior. The tribal casino is higher yet, hidden by a mass of willow brush as it stands across State Highway 13, behind the house and a few hundred yards to the southwest. From where I am, I face east and look down upon the reservation's dance grounds. Its bright green grassy circle is bathed in morning sunlight.

This is the weekend of the Fourth of July. The tribe's annual pow wow is about to begin. The vendors' sales stands, most with canopies, are in place. An even dozen, they form an outer ring around the spot of grass. Their centripetal orientation is striking, directed inward like that of circled wagons. Everything on or near the dance grounds is focused on the circle's center. It holds the ring of eight-foot-high white cedar posts with their cedar bought *ramada*. In the shade are the four drums. Their microphones stand next to them, their black rubber electrical cords lying like spilled spaghetti on the grass. The male drummers — who also are the singers — are seated around them, each holding a single drumstick.

This is a *traditional* pow wow. This means certain important things that often go unregistered by non-tribal onlookers. A fire is kindled and kept burning throughout the weekend of dancing. There is tobacco. Prayers are offered, and as is usually the case these days, no alcohol or other drugs are evident. Most of this goes unvoiced, but is carefully planned, and the required rituals are quietly tended to by the event's overseers.

The dancers, in their colorful regalia, are lined up outside the grounds on the east side, toward the lake. They fall in behind the lead dancers who are behind the staff bearers. The feathered staffs are held prominently beside the bright cloth of Old Glory. The black and white flag meant to call our attention to those still missing in Vietnam is also present. These staffs, banners, and people await the call of the drum for the grand entry. But first the fire must be tended, the tobacco put down, the words said. The appointed fire watcher leans at his task, the barely discernible wisp of airy blue smoke rising before him. A team of watchers will assure that the fire keeps burning until the last drum has departed sometime late on Sunday.

Today the sky is a deep blue with only a few white cumulus clouds out over the lake's channel. They are moving away, to the east. Here the prevailing wind comes out of the west. Basswood Island, colored a deep green, rests in the lake as if waiting to hear the drum. It has witnessed this scene many times. There are other witnesses.

Beside the dance ground, on the north side, is the white cement block building that was the Catholic grade school for years, and a smaller flat-topped garage-like structure. Now both stand empty. On their west side is the two storied white block apartment building in which the single remaining nun lives, her footsteps loud in the almost empty halls. In the past it was the home of the resident priest and several nuns. Most of that is over.

Across the street, in a cluster of tall spruce trees, is the white clapboard church, its back turned to the lake, a small gold cross at its peak only a few feet taller than the trees. Soon the green spruces will tower above it. People will come to the call of the church bell on Sunday morning, filing in for Mass, but they will be few compared to those on the dance ground. The tingling of the bells at Mass will be heard inside the church as will those outside, on the ankles of dancers. This weekend the drum will be the center of attention.

The bell, the steeple, and its small wooden roof with black

asphalt shingles, now rests on the lawn at the north side of the church's high concrete front steps. A short rope dangles from it, easily moved by the wind. To me, a steeple-less church seems deeply inadequate, and perhaps serves to symbolize a serious diminishment. Whenever I come upon the scene it appears that the church has been decapitated, its steeple cut off and left to fall onto the earth nearby. There no longer is a tall church spire at Red Cliff that reaches up to the Christian heavens. Now, it sits solidly upon the earth, at human eye level, and in this way it is like today's nearby pow wow drums. They, too, rest directly upon the earth, are in the very midst of the people who gather around them. I see the lowered church bell and spire suggesting that perhaps heaven is not so distant after all; that maybe it was here on this wooded shoreline all along.

Along with the uncle's house a few other structures stand more distant from the dance ground. The tribe's tourist park lies to the east, in the aspen grove beside the lake. It is filled this weekend with tents and trailers of pow wow attendees. Licence plates tell of Canadian, Michigan, and Minnesotan families—mostly Ojibwe—who make this annual trek to Red Cliff. Ho-Chunk and Menominee from southern and central Wisconsin also come. And the Odawa, Potawatomi, Dakota, and Lakota Nations are represented. This pow wow is more than a homecoming for Red Cliff people. It is an international gathering.

Then comes the loud call of the drum. The dancers start their entry. I cross the road and walk down to join them.

Pow wows have become part of my life. After a childhood and youth without them, I suddenly was caught in their grasp. Once you break through you have to love them. But it all takes time. You may not be able to come from the outside and immediately feel the drumbeat deep in your soul. Perhaps you have to be prepared for it by other revelations. Maybe you have to have learned that there is something more.

It has been said that the pow wow drum and its accompanying singers use notes that we whites cannot hear. That could be;

it certainly would help explain the seemingly absolute disinterest so many of my non-Ojibwe relatives and friends show toward Indian things. To be involved in Native America in Lake Superior Country is to be involved in pow wows. (Not all tribes have the sort of dance gatherings I am calling pow wows here.) But certainly in any European-American's past there were drums. I'm not referring to the martial drumbeats of the last few hundred years, those of such wrath and destruction. I'm asking you to think back much further, back thousands and thousands of years. Did the Neanderthal peoples have music? Did they sing and dance? Did they hear a drumbeat? I surely hope so. How could humans live without these things?

So perhaps the reason I cannot hear all the notes used by a pow wow's musicians today is because I have been so long without them. Maybe, in time, I will hear them. Anyway, the drumbeat that moves through me when at a pow wow is enough for now. How could there be more?

For some of us the beat of the pow wow drum might have an immediate effect. It resonates with the beat inside our chests so it holds us from the start. When circling around the drum we are pulled into it. We move beyond ourselves.

In one way or another the beat of a drum has always been heard at Red Cliff. I say that with a good deal of certainty, but with a good deal of assumption as well. Certainty and assumption go together, until, perhaps, they become each other. The "heathenish dances" I have already mentioned taking place on the Red Cliff shoreline in the 1820's must have been part of a long history of such gatherings because Ojibwe people have been on Lake Superior's south shore for hundreds of years. And as I also have already said, there were other tribesmen before them. We're talking thousands of years here. That's how long the Red Cliff woods has heard the beat of the drum.

So Red Cliff is familiar with drums and pow wows. (The word pow wow, by the way, supposedly goes back to colonial times in North America when the European used it to identify tribal religious leaders.) It seems religion and the drum have been together from the start. For the last twenty-three years the reservation has held a traditional pow wow on the weekend of the Fourth of July. It's a celebration of independence. One must wonder about that. Independence from England? Or twenty-three years ago, in 1977, with its first of these recent pow wows, was the community telling of an independence of another sort?

At all the Red Cliff pow wows I have attended, I noticed how few non-Indians were present. People from the nearby towns of Bayfield, Cornucopia, Washburn, and Ashland seemed to be few in numbers. Several years ago, I sat in the shade of a vendor's canopy just outside the dance ring. He was white and his wife was a Canadian Ojibwe. The couple and the woman's sister had driven down to Red Cliff from their Canadian homes. While this man and I sat and talked, the two women were with the other dancers, moving around the dance ring. They were the only women with jingle dresses and they easily caught the attention of everyone present. This was in the times when these old *medicine* dresses were only starting to come back. I inquired just how he made the glistening, curved metal cones that covered his wife's dress and he gladly showed me. This man told how his relatives—all in the Twin Cities area—"didn't understand this," as he waved a hand out to the dancers. Perhaps that's why so few whites attend these dances. Maybe they don't understand.

One of the most important pow wows I have attended took place back in 1993. For years I had concluded that as Native Americans the Crow people were among the tribes that have stood firm over the years. They lived adjacent to the Little Bighorn site of the famous 1876 battle in which George Armstrong Custer died. I wanted to drive out west for the Crow Fair for a long time, and somehow I was finally able to arouse interest in several Red Cliff relatives. We rented a large van, and one early August morning we were on the highway, heading west.

It was exciting to be with these travelers, some of whom rarely left Northern Wisconsin. As we entered western Minnesota and the expanse of the prairie opened up, I was interested in their reactions to all the space. These were people from the wooded shoreline of Lake Superior. Geography's often unstated effect on humans interests me. It can be an unrecognized variable that helps drive a people's world view. It was not a little thing for us to suddenly, on a clear summer morning, leave the cover of the woods and enter a boundless plain. At least this change would be erased by being with family.

Except for the rest stop at Wall, South Dakota, and another at Deadwood, we made only two major stops on the way out. The group readily agreed to stop at Crazy Horse Mountain and Mount Rushmore. At Crazy Horse, we were pleased that except for the two white faces in the van, all others were recognized as Native Americans and, therefore, admitted without charge. The Crazy Horse stop was powerful. We quietly pondered the concerns of some Lakota voices that said the sculpture should not have been attempted, that it was antithetical to the spirituality of the man, Crazy Horse. You don't make a showpiece of someone as important as Crazy Horse, this voice says. Perhaps we wanted to see what this was all about.

Even though the monument was not completed, we were awed by it. These Ojibwe came and paid their respect. We spoke little of it, our thoughts seemingly better kept inside. But one utterance stays with me. It came from my wife, who rarely speaks of these sorts of things. As we stood on the viewing deck, facing the mountain where the image of Crazy Horse and his powerful four-legged companion were beginning to take form, she said quietly, "It makes you proud you're an Indian."

That warm summer morning we went from the wonder of the unfinished Crazy Horse monument directly to Mount Rushmore. Most of the members of our small entourage had not been there before. Unlike at Crazy Horse, we were met with an almost immaculately trimmed and polished venue. This was big-time tourism, I told myself. This was a serious and obviously orchestrated patriotism. Filled by a flowing throng of tourists, Mount Rushmore, in its obviously orchestrated pretentiousness was miles and miles from Crazy Horse. Rushmore had an air of hurried festiveness. Lines formed outside the restrooms. The gift shop shelves were filled and their cash registers were obviously heated. The smooth blacktopped walkway leading up to the viewing areas was colonnaded with waving colorful cloth flags from the world's nations. I searched for flags of aboriginal nations but found none.

The four famous stone faces stared out of the rock, all without smiles — businesslike. I stood and stared. Try as I might, I could not push the image of Sitting Bull from my mind. The famous Lakota leader was invisible, but as clearly evident as the stone faces. He stood directly behind these national culture heroes. His message was as loud as the greatest South Dakota thunderstorm. Our group walked away from Mount Rushmore in silence.

The Crow Fair is one of the largest tribal celebrations on the continent. Held at Crow Agency in Montana, it draws thousands of participants. Horse races, competitive dancing, the popular grand entry of the numerous Crow clans with their elaborately decorated horses are all part of the attraction. There are food vendors and the usual crafts people. A village of a few hundred large teepees is erected for many of the visitors and participants. It is true spectacle on the hot Northern Plains.

We found the tribe's offices in the town of Crow Agency and introduced ourselves. We were greeted cordially and assisted in finding lodging. We watched the dancers, sat through the long giveaway ceremony, enjoyed Indian tacos, and even tried the tripe soup. We bought beaded jewelry.

We marveled at the Crow youngsters riding bareback on their sleek, energetic horses. Each day they came through the parking areas, around the vehicles, along the dirt roads. And we visited with the people: Arapaho, Cheyenne, Lakota, Blackfeet, Piegan, Ute, Shoshoni, Sarsee, and Crow.

The names jumped off the pages of school books. These plains people welcomed us. "Ojibwe?," they asked. "Oh yes. Lake Superior." The names jumped off the pages of schoolbooks. And the dancers' clothing was striking—so colorful! But amidst all this it was the drums that held us. The drum groups were numerous, their high pitched songs new to our ears. This was a new kind of Indian Country for most of us, and we were held, made welcome by the strong call of the drums.

Later when we visited the Custer site and stood outside the black wrought iron fence to view the markers where soldiers had fallen, we stood in silence. Why had these intruders come? What assumptions were they living under? The park ranger who spoke inside the new interpretive center told of the many European immigrant men who, often out of financial need, joined the US Army soon after coming across the ocean, to be given inadequate training before being whisked out west "to fight Indians." These men barely spoke English, some not at all, They fumbled, ineptly, with their unfamiliar rifles. The nearby cemetery gave their foreign names.

The trip back home offered time for telling of what we had seen. We talked of the Crow. We spoke again of the horses, the many dancers, and of the huge giveaway that went on for hours. Our Red Cliff pow wow was small in comparison.

On the long drive back to Northern Wisconsin, I was hoping for one last stop: Mandan, North Dakota. Today, the Mandan people sometimes come to us in the paintings of George Catlin. This tribe is known for its elaborate, ceremonial and artistic expression and for having suffered a devastating smallpox epidemic.

It was to Mandan Country that the U.S. Army brought Chief Joseph and his several hundred people as captives in 1877. They were incarcerated at Fort Lincoln in Mandan before being moved south. I wanted to see how today's Mandan, North Dakota told all that. But this stop was not to be. We all were tired and uncomfortable in the cramped van. A brother-in-law taking his turn at the wheel did not turn off the interstate at Mandan. "Enough of this sightseeing," he said. "We're going home."

But perhaps the most intriguing pow wow I attended at Red Cliff took place in the early 1970's on a warm summer evening at Raspberry Bay. The mosquitos, dusk, the drum, the Odanah drum— the informal gathering under the pines.

This was in those times after the last of Red Cliff's open public pow wows of the early 1900's and before their re-establishment in the 1970's. This was an informal gathering under the pines in Raspberry Campground. Without a noticeable white presence, this was just for The People. An Odanah drum was set up, the high-pitched voices of its singers resonating through the trees.

Reservation residents gathered under the pines, leaning on their pickup trucks and automobiles. In between songs, quiet chatter and laughter were heard. Laid back and comfortable, this gathering was, I concluded, what had always gone on in these woods. It had not died. And not many years after this quiet affair, Red Cliff once again had its own big drum. The circle had come 'round.

Since that time in Raspberry, there have been many other pow wows for me. Some have been huge; some small. some have been in great new convention centers in large cities and some were held outside under the treets. At a small pow wow just south of Milwaukee, I stood in the food line next to Iron Eyes Cody. We talked easily about the day. At another native gathering several years later in Eau Claire, I enjoyed roasted buffalo cut from a shank and cooked on a spit over an open fire just outside the dance circle. One hot August night in South Dakota, I was honored to help out at a Sun Dance. Then, once in New Hampshire, I danced the Veteran's Dance with the Mohawk, Miemac and Penobscot.

In 1995, the Red Cliff pow wow honored a set of my wife's grandparents. Both gone, this couple lived in the village through most of the twentieth century.

Their descendents, my extended family of in-laws, were asked to provide a feast and giveaway at the weekend gathering. For months meetings were held, plans were discussed, items accumulated. Relatives from Canada took part, providing a large amount of moose meat. Others from distant states came home to help. There was venison, wild rice, and fry bread. At the feast—open to all comers—over five hundred people were fed. The giveaway was the same.

The family called out the names of persons who came up for their items, and finally everyone on the pow wow grounds was asked to come forward to be given things. At the conclusion the family was honored with its own honor dance. In step with the loud drumbeat, we led the dancers around the ring.

I was pleased to notice our oldest son out in front, bent at the waist, lifting his feet carefully, his arms bent upward as he led us. It had been years since he danced—in adulthood he came to favor a life in the city—but there he was back on the pow wow grounds, looking as if he had never left.

Importantly, at Red Cliff and the other Ojibwe reserves, more and more the Anishinaabe language, *Ojibwemowin,* is heard along with the drum. As a tribal member recently told me: "The people are starting to learn who they are."

Last year, on the Sunday of pow wow weekend I went back to our Frog Creek cabin a bit early, leaving the dance grounds before dark. Much later, just as darkness fell, I heard the fast and loud drum beat signaling the end of the pow wow. The drum was over four miles away. I sat in the cabin by oil lamp and imagined its sound waves coming through the trees. This is the way it used to be, I thought. Over the years Elders had told me that it was common to hear the drum sounding though the reservation from spring into fall.

But pow wows are not for everyone, not even for all Indian people. There are those at Red Cliff to prefer other things, finding some place out of town to be on the 4th of July weekend. I have not heard it said openly, but at first, in the years when the pow wow was just getting started, there was a feeling that a traditional pow wow was not wanted. It's like the remark an older reservation man said to me back in the late 1960's. We were working in a rhubarb patch, earning a few dollars cutting rhubarb for a local fruit grower. One of my brother-in-laws had recently let his hair grow long and he was wearing it in a pony tail. The elderly man asked me about it, wondering why he was not getting it cut. Then he said, "He's setting the Indian back ten years!"

The legacy of years of pressures to assimilate into the greater society is still evident at Red Cliff. Usually, this is not something openly talked about. The deeply important things rarely are. This is an attitude the early pow wows had to deal with. But over the twenty-three years changes have been witnessed. The older couple that who used to leave town on pow wow weekend now stays home. Last July I visited with both of them in the pow wow bleachers. They do not dance, but they have found some comfort in being with the crowd, enjoying some fry bread. They have come round.

For the last two decades, the reservation has held a traditional pow wow on the weekend of the Fourth of July. Perhaps it's a celebration of independence. One must wonder about that. Independence from what? Colonial England? Or in 1977, with the first of these recent pow wows, was the community telling of an independence of another sort?

Last fall on the first weekend in October my wife and I drove up to Red Cliff for the weekend. While she visited with the relatives I spent most of Saturday and Sunday out in our cabin. It was the weekend of Bayfield's Fall Apple Festival. I rarely go into town for this event, preferring instead the solitude of the woods. But this time I was to walk out on Sunday and drive into town to pick up a few family members after the parade that was the finale of the weekend's reveling.

So, dutifully, I closed up the cabin and walked out to the truck parked at the trail head. The weekend was over. It was to be the familiar four hour drive back to the city. Coming to Bayfield from the north, I was lucky to find a parking spot up on the hillside distant from main street. I parked, locked the Jeep, and began the descent into town. A few blocks away I heard the start of sirens. These were from four or five fire and rescue vehicles that concluded the parade. Their loud wailing did not cease. It had to be twenty minutes, at least. Only at the end of the parade route were the sirens silenced.

Down on the main street, I joined the crowd. Paper and Styrofoam cups and aluminum cans and plastic bottles tumbled from trash containers. Discarded scraps of paper and plastic blew in the wind. Some of the watchers were drunk after the weekend of partying.

Across the street from where I stood, I noted the colorful neon signs in a tavern window. In the late afternoon shade, they were bright as beacons: Budweiser, Miller High Life, Summit. Glancing at a side street, I saw a vendor's booth with bulky wool sweaters from Ecuador. Another offered only Christmas tree ornaments. A third displayed acrylic paintings of the Lake Superior shore line. All were labeled—one telling the viewer, he or she, was looking at a painting of the "Red Rocks of Squaw Bay." These were rendered by an artist from a posh suburb of Minneapolis.

I noted that some of the vendors that lined the sidewalks were packing their wares, preparing to move on to the next fall festival. Turning to view the alley directly behind me, I saw a sleek, cherry-black Lexus sedan parked in the owner's spot behind a main street fudge shop. The license plate facing me showed the blue waters of Minnesota's 10,000 lakes.

Then, finally, came the last units of the parade. The insistently overbearing, loud wailing fire and rescue vehicles — both from Red Cliff and Bayfield — passed. They were followed by the colorful high school marching band made up of all the school bands that took part in the parade. This huge group seemed to be trying to outdo the fire and rescue vehicles in raising the town's decibel level. Now, without their cumbersome and often hot band uniform jackets, each student wore bright red Apple Festival Parade T-shirts given by parade officials. The youthful musicians' faces told of pleasure in realizing that in less than a minute it would all be over.

Another celebration—another pow wow—I thought. Then, as this large and composite high school band passed, the crowd spilled into the street and I was left standing alone amidst the litter at the curb. For a few troubling moments, I wondered where I was.

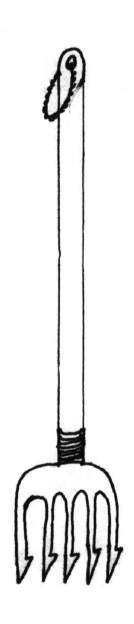

Empty Nets

At Red Cliff the tradition of taking fish from Lake Superior is ancient. This way of life is a strong thread that stretches back to the unrecorded past. Fishing is one of the realities that help to shape the reservation's deep orientation to the lake. It is stitched into the fabric of the community's identity.

This was acknowledged by the Wisconsin Supreme Court in 1972, when the court wrote:

"The history of the Chippewa (Ojibwe) reveals an uninterrupted history of fishing on Lake Superior. They have occupied the land in what is now Bayfield and Ashland counties for more than 300 years... (And thus)... They have been fishing in Lake Superior continually since the sixteenth or seventeenth century."

But through most of the last one hundred years, reservation people fished under conditions of almost unbelievable repression. During these years the setting and lifting of nets was usually done secretively, under cover of darkness. In the past, people have been jailed for fishing at Red Cliff, yet through all of these hard times they continued to go to the lake.

Why did the people have to fish this way?

The Red Cliff Ojibwe felt their fishing in Lake Superior was guaranteed by the treaties their ancestors signed with the federal government in 1837, 1842 and 1854. That this fishing was being carried out in the early days just after the treaty-signing is shown by remarks about Red Cliff by the Commissioner of Indian Affairs in 1861:

"This reserve being located on the lake, where there is an abundance of fish the entire year, and being under the immediate supervision of the agent, the Indians who are located thereon are the most comfortable of any within this agency."

This long sentence tells us two things. The first is that the people fished all year, not just during the state's imposed seasons for sport anglers. In the 1860's the lake was playing a major role in providing food for the people. The second thing the quotation says is that in 1861 Red Cliff people were living "under the immediate supervision of the agent." Immediate? Did he dictate their every move?—Their every motivation? The Office of the Commissioner of Indian Affairs at the time apparently felt that it and its field agents were to take the credit for the well being of the reserve's people. Federal Indian policy was working.

Perhaps a more creditable view would be that the people were, in 1861, by and large, taking care of themselves. Their old subsistence patterns, including the fishing of *Gichigami* in all seasons, was still doing them well. In other words, while the "greater" society felt it was the reason for the well-being of the Indian, it was the native people, doing their own things, that were behind their well being.

The archives go on to tell us that Red Cliff people were enjoying a degree of success as commercial fishermen in the late 1800's. Here is what an Office of Indian Affairs Report for 1891 says about it:

"The waters of the lake yield a bountiful supply of excellent fish and the surplus catch and all other surplus products find a ready market in the city of Bayfield. In capturing the fish both gill and pound nets are employed. The natives own a small fleet of sailboats, and in navigating their little craft they display the confidence and skill of experienced sailors."

But in the 1880's and 1890's, a burgeoning non-Indian commercial fishing industry headquartered at both the western and southern boundaries of the reserve—at Cornucopia and Bayfield appeared. There was competition.

Voices started to be heard that claimed the Indians were taking too much of the catch. Under this pressure, the State of Wisconsin acted. In 1897, its appointed authorities decreed that Red Cliff's Ojibwe had to abide by the state's fishing regulations. The "old" treaties were deemed to be superseded by state law. After this legal decision, reservation people began to be jailed for fishing out of the state's sport season. When found by state wardens, Indian nets were confiscated, sometimes burned on the spot. Any tribal commercial fishing was effectively stopped, but subsistence fishing continued, usually under cover of darkness. From 1897 to 1972—for seventy-five years—Red Cliff continued to go to the lake but risked being arrested for doing it.

I have been part of numerous fishing excursions on the reservation and have collected recountings of many more. One that stands out took place in 1965. It was a trip to Raspberry Bay to raise a net that a brother-in-law had set the night before. To me the trip stands as an instance of determined self-expression. It was autumn and the lake trout were running up into the shallower waters. It was time to go out after them. That's what the people had always done.

We left the house in early morning, just as the glow of the new sun lit the night sky over Basswood Island. I drove my dark green Volkswagen Beetle from the yard and decided to switch on the headlights. It was still that dark. Soon, along the blacktopped roadway, we came upon the figure of an uncle returning from a night in town, an opened six-pack under an arm. He climbed into the back seat.

We turned off the blacktop reservation road north of the village, onto the dirt road leading down to Raspberry Campground. Now a large imposing green and white wooden hand-painted sign stands at that corner telling viewers that this is a private campground, open only to tribal members. That morning it was just an unmarked corner in the forest; a quiet junction of two relatively unused paths, one modernized, the other not.

It's at the river that my memory is more complete. The campground was and still is "undeveloped." Tribal members use it mostly during the summer. It sits on a peninsula formed by a curve in the Raspberry River as it winds its quiet way through the forest to Lake Superior. Large pine trees—white and red—cover the area. Their pleasing canopy guards the earth beneath them, where blueberry, trailing arbutus, wintergreen, and moccasin flowers find nutrition in its sandy soil. Their lower branches have been trimmed away, so at a human's eye level the area is open.

It's a special place, known to other tribal people who occasionally visit Red Cliff. Oftimes, it is their private campground, hidden away from whites. The good feeling of a sanctuary comes to me when I'm there, and the sandy pathways under the trees have a welcome, alluring pull. In the past I have driven over them carefully, imagining my wheels sinking down and spinning, only to sink further and further as in quicksand. Yet the paths hold and provide traction. I imagine the trails under the pines, amongst the northern boreal ground cover plants as eager to pull me into them, appealing to my urge to become part of the peninsula, to blend with its naturalness. This imagery—of being overwhelmed by the purity of nature—is a recurrent one when I visit the campground.

This net checking took place on an October morning. I parked the Beetle at the landing. My brother-in-law untied the aging wooden rowboat pulled up into the few cattails that grew in that spot. The uncle, his opened six-pack still under an arm, took the bow seat, my brother-in-law sat amidships with the single homemade basswood oar, and I sat in the stern. We pushed off and turned the boat downstream.

I recall that my two partners carried on an active conversation, mostly about what went on in town the night before. They ignored the city dweller at the back of the boat. I had, by this time, given up my Saturday night revelling, and thus became uninteresting company on Sunday mornings.

As the quiet but lively banter ensued, talk about who was seen downtown, who did what and said what, I studied the river. It was an unseasonably warm October morning, the warmth matched by the stillness. There was not the hint of a breeze, and the river's movement was difficult to detect. The only ripples were caused by the crude oar and the minor wake from our boat. It was as if the water were a solid instead of a liquid and we were slowly poling our way over the buoyant mass.

An enticing veil of morning fog lay here and there on the river, never with enough substance to block the view, but just enough to add a welcome mysticism to the scene. It was the sort of ethereal fog, similar in this way to the night's lingering remnants, that would instantly be burned away by the early sun's rays. The shores of the river were lined with orange and red maples, yellow aspens, and dark emerald hemlocks, balsams, spruces, and pines.

The scene had a presence. It was beyond mere water, trees, sky and air. It had gone beyond the confines of its own physical being into something more. Such a morning, I concluded, was not for mortals. We were venturing out onto a river, a river in the forest of the center of the universe. I imagined the mythical *manidoog* perched among the branches along the shores, silently watching us move by. They clustered among the bright oranges and reds, were scattered in the yellows of the aspens, and found spaces to rest on the branches of the large hemlocks. These other-than-human persons lived in this silent place, and they were sleepily letting us enter their realm.

The Ojibwe trickster, *Wenabozo,* must have been there, too, but you often are not sure of his presence. His ability to change forms—his ability to transform himself into almost anything— means he could have been the aging pine stump we passed, or the dark sandstone rocks that lay protruding from the stump's dead roots in the red clay banks.

After long moments of this reverie, I was brought back by the sound of a near empty beer can hitting the still surface of the river. Soon I passed it as it sat jauntily, like a drunken sailor, upright in the water. My first urge was to reach out and take it into the boat, for it did not belong in this pristine place, but my arm did not move. My anthropological training told me not to intrude, not to bring my values into this place. The can remained standing on the water, slowly tipping from side to side in our lazy wake. Immediately the pop of the opening of one of its full companions was heard. The uncle was still thirsty.

And so we slowly made our way along the river to its mouth at Raspberry Bay. The morning's silence competed with the continuing chatter and occasional laughter of my two companions. More muffled splats were heard as more cans hit the water. More pops, until, upon reaching the river's mouth I turned and saw four beer cans, plus the torn cardboard carton that had held them, all floating at ease on the water in a staggered line along the mile or so to the lake.

The river was at peace. The busy summer had ended and the stillness of autumn was its fresh replacement. The harshness of winter's sleep was in the offing, but this morning was the pause before all that. Betwixt and between. That's what spring and fall are. They are liminal times, sacred times between the often frenetic life of summer and the resting time of winter.

We rounded a tiny curve and suddenly the vast openness of the big lake burst upon us. We were in Raspberry Bay. Here the water was so clear and still that we immediately saw the bottom drop away to a depth of ten or fifteen feet. We quickly found the nylon net. It hung, suspended just beneath the water's surface, anchored by a few lines tied to rocks dropped to the bottom, and held up by colored plastic floats, the size of hot dog buns, tied onto the net's topmost strand. It was suspended in the unmoving water as if held by invisible arms safely out of the sight of distant passersby, not easily detected by the state's game wardens. An anchoring line, attached to the top corner nearest shore, led underwater until only a few yards from the sandy beach to a white birch, and was tied low at ground level.

The net was set to be barely detectable from the water. Only the anchoring shoreline told of its presence, and this was noticeable only to an experienced searcher. This was in the years before the court victory in a case to test tribal fishing rights, so the net was set in its hidden fashion so that the state game wardens who sometimes patrolled these waters at night would miss it. The tribesmen, whose relatives had fished these waters for over two hundred years were, since the State of Wisconsin ruling in 1997, legally unable to fish in the traditional way, in all times on open water, except during the state's sport fishing seasons. We saw immediately that the net was empty. Then we spotted a few dead suckers, lying on the bottom, directly below the net. Apparently they had been removed from the net and left to sink. The lake trout we expected were not found. Someone had lifted the net and emptied it before our arrival.

There was no need for us to lift the net, so we left it in place and slowly began our trip back up the river. By now the vestiges of night had left. We passed the carton and cans one by one, my companions unconcerned about them as they speculated about who had taken the fish. It was the time of year for the trout to run and several of them should have been in the net. I thought of *Wenabozo*. It was the sort of trick he would pull.

Other than quiet speculation about who the thief was, the return was uneventful. My companions were not angry. They accepted the fact of the empty net, and after its short discussion, put the matter aside.

On the trip back I absorbed the colors and smells of the morning as I did on the trip to the bay. Sunday morning silence on a colorful October day, in the deep woods. I saw the beer cans, but tried not to. They had been carried downstream a bit and were out of reach from our path up the center of the river.

I thought, too, of the people who in the early decades of the century had lived in this spot. Now, no one lived here permanently except the *manidoog*. I imagined the bark wigwams, the tarpaper-covered wooden board houses that were the homes of the early people.

Despite the passing of the years, perhaps little has changed.

The river was still there; some of the bordering trees still turned
to light colors in the fall. And Red Cliff people were still netting
in Raspberry Bay.

There was another noteworthy fishing incident that I was
part of. This happened in the fall of 1969. This time a net had
been set in Buffalo Bay. Its lifting was the occasion of some
concern. My wife, our two children and I were living in Superior, almost seventy miles away. We knew of the importance of
this event, so arrangements were made to be released from our
work duties for the day. We rose early, bundled up the youngsters and drove to Red Cliff.

The 1960's were a time of much political unrest in Indian
Country. Red Cliff had its share of this. We knew there was talk
of the community's legal right to harvest fish from the lake without regard to laws of the State of Wisconsin. There was a growing sentiment of sovereignty. In an attempt at an earlier test
case, lake trout had been taken and a publicized attempt was
made to market them, but this was not accomplished. No one
would buy the fish.

Finally, with the promise of legal assistance from the federal
program entitled Judicare, other plans were made. A fish net
was to be set in the lake at Red Cliff and lifted simultaneously
with an instance of "illegal" deer hunting at the St. Croix Ojibwe
community located further inland in northwest Wisconsin. We
knew about this and waited to be informed of the day these two
events were to occur. Finally the word came.

Philip Gordon, the Red Cliff tribal chairman at the time,
notified a local television station about the pending net lifting,
asking that the story be held until the following day. It was not
held and the day before the net was to be lifted the law enforcement officers swooped down onto the reservation in droves. For
this case to be carried out properly, a net needed to be set, but
there was fear that the law enforcement presence in the community would curtail the setting before it took place. Finally,
after nightfall, when the authorities tired and left for their beds,

two Red Cliff men rowed out into Buffalo Bay — at 3 a.m. — and successfully set the net.

When we arrived in the community a small crowd had already gathered at the dock at Buffalo Bay. About thirty or so tribal people showed, some carrying hand-lettered signs shouting to whomever would listen about the tribe's "rights" to take the fish. One sign said simply "Indian Uprising."

At the appointed time, a State of Wisconsin Department of Natural Resources boat appeared from the south and held a position off shore. Then came the net lifting. Six Red Cliff men climbed into two rowboats and rowed out to the spot of the net and lifted it to the cheers of those of us on shore. As soon as the net was free from the water and placed into one of the boats the Wisconsin authorities came alongside. The six net lifters were placed under arrest, taken into the larger boat, their rowboats towed to shore.

Ironically the net was empty except for a lone sucker. And interestingly, when the net was placed into the boat the portion with the unwanted fish was left hanging over the gunwale. On the way back to shore the fish fell back into the lake.

So once again I was witness to an empty net. But unlike at Raspberry Bay back in 1965, this empty net lead to something important. That morning the six men were taken into Bayfield to the Coast Guard Station where they were detained temporarily before being taken the eleven miles to Washburn, to the county courthouse. Here they were booked and charged with fishing out of season, then released upon the payment of bail. None of them spent a night in jail. The case worked its way through to Judge Voight, who finally ruled in favor of the Ojibwe.

This is known as the Gurnoe Decision, or the Voight Case. It ended the seventy-five years of illegal control over Red Cliff fishing.

Today one of our sons regularly spears fish at the Lac Courte Orielles Ojibwe community an hour south of Red Cliff. He does this on tribal waters as well as those off the reservation. He can harvest this resource from lands his ancestors ceded away in treaties because of the six Red Cliff men arrested in 1969.

The symbolism of nets is well known. The word *entanglement* and the phrase *cast a wide net* conjure familiar images. Then there is the thought of *an empty net.* It is this notion of emptiness, of lost opportunity, even of defeat that visits me this morning. I have had two experiences with empty nets at Red Cliff. Both are meaningful. One led to my better understanding of human behavior, of how acceptance can replace anger. The other led to a major federal court decision that helped right a wrong that had stood for much too long.

Joe Attikoosh

Our intent was to attend midnight Mass. It was the late 1970's and such a ceremony was still held at Red Cliff. Those who were interested in it told of going as youngsters, long ago. Sometimes, they said the church was filled with people. They liked to tell of those times when the hush of the season was over the church, when the strong sweet smelling incense stung their nostrils. But first we had to make a trip way out to Eagle Bay. We were taking Joe Attikoosh to the trail leading to the sugarbush.

Marlene drove our 1970 brown Dodge Dart carefully along the snow-covered roadways. We were miles away from any houses, and the thought of slipping into the ditch was not a pleasant one. The headlights' beams showed us that the ditches held some snow. Even though they were not level with the roadbed, we saw that they still held enough to make it impossible to get out without help. She drove the small Dodge with deliberation but still kept up some speed because of Mass. She did not want to be late. Her mother sat in the front seat beside her. I was in the back with Joe.

He had asked me to come with him and I was tempted to agree. The sugarbush cabin would have been an interesting place to spend the night. The barrel stove and the oil lamps would have afforded comfort in the dark winter woods. Surely he would have talked. Joe had had a near lifetime of experiences that I was eager to learn about. But for some reason I was uneasy. I was unprepared—without proper clothing, no flashlight and other "essentials." I did not accept the offer, and today, some twenty-five years later, I regret the decision.

At the trail head Joe stepped out into the darkness. Then, with the side door still open, he reached back into the seat beside me for his .22 caliber rifle and a small burlap sack. He wore oiled leather boots, heavy dark green woolen pants, an aging thick brown cotton mackinaw, and a faded red wool toque. He was in his late fifties and had spent a lifetime in these woods. He knew the trail well.

I still carry the image of his thin figure, of medium height, the burlap sack fastened with a length of wash line cord tossed over a shoulder. He cradled the old rifle in his left arm. I rolled the window down and he turned to the car and said a single quiet "Migweech." Then he faced the woods as he began to move down the trail. As Marlene stepped on the accelerator and the car slowly moved forward, I shouted a "Merry Christmas!" out to him and he waved an arm in reply before his dark figure was gone. It was December 24th, Christmas Eve.

Joe Attikoosh. Who was this man? For years I have been thinking of him. What is it that keeps him in my memory? His family name is on a few of the reservation's cemetery stones. I have found it in tribal papers. Over a hundred years ago it was common on the reservation. Today no one in Red Cliff carries it.

Back in the 1960's and 1970's our youngest son, Keller, was a toddler. He, Joe, and I would often spend hours together on our family's frequent trips home. Joe Attikoosh was someone I felt the boy had to get to know. Today, now facing his thirtieth year, his memories of Joe are limited, but he does remember him.

Some of Joe's friends called him "A'beese." An affectionate nickname, it seems to have been a rendering of an *Ojibwemowin* suffix marking the diminutive. Joe's father's name was also Joe. So the Joe Attikoosh I knew—in Anglicized form, was "Joe Jr."

A'beese, in the Ojibwe language, might have meant "Little Joe" or "Small Joe." He had many friends and "A'beese" is still spoken of with affection. People liked him.

But in traditional Ojibwe culture the names of the deceased, especially of those who recently died, are not to be spoken aloud, or if done so, ideally only in a ceremonial context. To use the name of such a person is to call spiritual attention to him or her. They might hear, and they might come a'calling. It is felt that sometimes the spirits of the recently deceased become lonely. They come back to take others along with them, for good company.

So I write of Joe Attikoosh with some trepidation. But I know he was a good man. Our times together were well spent. Besides, as I grow older there are times when I admit that I miss him.

Joe lived with the *mimigwesee*. These are, in English, "The Little People." Most world cultures have Little People. The Irish Leprechaun and the German Poltergeist come to mind. Sometimes, in the Christian world, angels are depicted in this miniature fashion. In the Ojibwe world, *mimigwesee* are powerful beings and deemed worthwhile, but there are taboos about spending too much time with them. There are taboos of avoidance.

Mimigwesee can paddle a canoe into a rock wall and disappear inside. They live in specified locations throughout the land. Joe knew where and he respected these places, even, at times, refused to travel through them. Today the Little People are still residing in the Red Cliff area. It must be somewhat difficult for them because of all the snowmobiles, all-terrain vehicles, kayaks, sailboats and other machines that sometimes allow even the most sacrosanct places to be violated.

Perhaps today Joe Attikoosh is at work, helping The Little People adapt to all this change. He knew the ways of the woods and the big lake. He knew the sky and its winds. He would be a big help to them.

When I first met Joe in 1960, he was a middle-age man who, to a great extent lived off the land. Always soft spoken, he asked for nothing. Even though there were few motor vehicles on the reservation in those days, he never asked me for a ride into town, or to go here or there. Cordial, he removed his cap in the presence of women. His face was darkened from a life outdoors. Always flushed, sometimes from wine drinking, it showed good color. His nose was slightly swollen from diabetes. Still, I felt he was pleasant to look at.

Joe was fluent in the language, but with the passing years he had few people to speak it with. But he came from a time when the speaking of Ojibwe was frowned upon. This was his mother tongue and is what he used as a child at home, but he was not to use it out in the world. He attended the Catholic grade school on the reservation and knew the sternness of the priests and nuns. So he adapted. It seemed to me that when in the woods, away from the village, Joe shucked something off, and smiled more. He lived in two worlds.

His houses were many. They were found here and there, wherever the seasons took him. Once, after the construction of the first tribal "housing project" he qualified for an apartment. My family and I were in Red Cliff for a weekend and I went looking for him. I found his unit in the project and knocked on the door. My son Keller, then three, was with me. Joe asked us in and we stepped up to the kitchen. Joe was baking bread, its welcome aroma filling the apartment. His furniture was sparse; the pieces given to him by friends left great spaces in the apartment's few rooms. The upstairs bedroom held only a small cot in a corner.

In those days some of the older men on the reservation were still scavenging old reservation dumping sites. They searched for anything having resale value, but looked especially for copper. A collection of salvaged copper wire, electric motor armitures and other pieces was piled just inside the door in the hallway. A hammer and screwdriver lay beside the pieces. Once collected the copper would be sold to an Ashland junk dealer.

After a cup of green tea—Joe apologized for not having any pop for Keller—we all took a ride into Bayfield. I had to stop at the grocery store for some things and Joe came in. He purchased a canned chicken. This was one of his favorites—a complete chicken in a can. Usually it went into a kettle of soup. Green tea, a chicken in a can, homemade bread, and "copper." In those worlds these were important to him.

The turn of the seasons lived through him. His life was still based on the age-old pattern of subsistence living found at Red Cliff in the 1800's. Bolstered with aspects of a cash economy, this cycle of activities continued to permeate the life ways of most reservation people during the entire twentieth century. There is the opinion that most of this is no longer found on the reservation—for example, see the 1998 report by Utah historian Dr. Anthony Godfrey on underwater logging on Red Cliff's shore line—but, in reality, this way of life is maintained by some reservation residents and is turned to by many others when in need.

Joe hunted, trapped, fished, and gathered plant food and medicines. As a child and youth he worked in his mother's sugarbush out at Frog Bay and later he became a mainstay in the Newago Sugarbush at Eagle Bay. Joe riced. Like many others, he regularly set nets all along the reservation shoreline. He usually had a chunk of venison in his possession, or knew where to get a deer in short order. He took ducks in fall and harvested other smaller game animals. He was an expert at finding and using wild plants for food, for medicine, and for manufacturing tools and other objects.

Long ago, one October day, Keller and I found him at his camp out at Raspberry River. Weeks earlier he told us he was living out there and that he was going to try to stay for the entire winter. On our next trip north we drove out to visit. A double track led through the thick woods just off the road going into Raspberry Campground. I steered our 1977 silver Chevrolet Impala down the track, moving slowly to navigate the sudden sharp turns. I hoped the branches that squeaked along the sides of the car did not leave marks. After a hundred yards or so we came into the clearing beside the river.

Joe was kneeling beside a small campfire, stirring something in a blackened frying pan. He had heard the car's engine's murmur and waved a dark metal spatula in greeting.

Joe was preparing to take his small wooden boat out on the river in search of ducks. But, graciously, he postponed the hunting trip and asked us to take seats around the fire. He offered us the remnants of his supper, a kettle of soup made from potatoes, white rice and portions of duck. Having just eaten, we declined. He heated tea.

Keller found a stick and poked at the fire a bit, then settled down on a large chunk of white birch used as a stool. He and I chatted with our friend, asking him how it was going "this fall." I recall that he told about recently returning from a trip with friends down to Lake Totogetic near Sealy, Wisconsin, to harvest wild rice, and that he said it would be good to "get a bear now" because they were "putting on their thick layers of fat." But mostly the three of us sat by the fire and enjoyed the evening. A few nights of early frost had solved the mosquito problem so we were comfortable. The maples and aspens beside the river were glorious and in the shadows of dusk the white birches in the clearing were becoming bright in a fuzzy way.

With cups of hot green tea in hand, we walked over to what Joe called his house. It was made of two old house doors, their white paint chipping away. They were nailed together on one side, then spread apart on the other. They were fastened to a wooden platform. One end was boarded up, the other covered with a small piece of heavy canvas. Inside was a single commercially-made mattress, its grey and white striped cover still showing some brightness. There was more than enough room for one person, and two could have spent the night rather comfortably.

"Which side does the girlfriend sleep on?" I kidded.

"Huh?" Joe grunted in surprise. "She's not fussy. She sleeps on either one or the other."

This small structure was his "house." Keller looked it over. To a youngster from the city it was interesting, indeed. Then he, at the time only four years old, said, "I like it. It's just big enough. It's like the tent we made when we built that fort."

Joe's "house" was built in the style used by Ojibwe people who spent a night or more out on a trap line in winter. I have heard of such structures hurriedly set up by Red Cliff men who would spend several days out on the islands bobbing for fish. During the day they would be on the ice, but at night they often stayed on an island, sleeping in these little enclosures. They were easily made of two notched saplings set into the snow or ground, then after a longer crosspiece was set in place, their sides and ends were layered with balsam and spruce boughs. I was told that if you built one big enough, and if you were very careful, there could be room for two people and a small fire between them.

That night at the river, Joe told us how he lived in a hut like this—only considerably bigger—all summer out on the islands. He claimed that it was at this very campground where he, as a young boy, with his father and mother, would push off in a large canoe or rowboat and spend the entire summer foraging on the different islands. "My dad hunted and my ma set nets," he said. "Usually we'd go out after maple sugar time. We lived that way until it got too cold. Then we'd pack up and come back for the winter. Sometimes we came back earlier in time for ricing."

"You mean you lived off of what you found out there?" I asked.

"Oh, we'd take some things along—flour, tea and coffee. We always had maple sugar we made. And my mother would take some cooking dishes. My dad had his gun and nets. It seemed we always came back with more than what we took. There was usually deer meat we'd bring back."

The Apostle Islands were used all year long by the Ojibwe. Some families would paddle or row out for blueberries, cranberries, and even the small wild strawberry. Groups of Ojibwe would go out to pick blueberries. They camped in the blueberry fields, selling the crated fruit to a buyer from Bayfield who came out in a large motorboat. Then there was the hunting and trapping that drew people out. And always there was the setting of fish nets. The islands still hold prime fishing grounds used by the people.

Joe Attikoosh remembered all this as if it had happened only yesterday. He recalled how sometimes small fires were set and let burn in order to try to encourage wild berries to spread and produce more prolifically.

We know that the Ojibwe insisted that the 1854 treaty held an article that allowed all this to continue. It tells how a portion of land on the far end of Madeline Island is reserved as a "fishing ground" for the Ojibwe. But I think the implication here is for more than fishing. I prefer to see the treaty guaranteeing the Ojibwe the perpetual use of all the islands for their seasonal hunting, fishing, and plant foraging activities.

But with the coming of the Apostle Island National Lakeshore much of this has been curtailed. "Confiscated for the greater national good," the Apostle Islands have—except for Madeline—been protected from development, but in the process the age-old subsistence practices of the local tribesmen have been detrimentally affected. Lake Superior's waters have been traversed by canoe and wooden rowboat by Red Cliff's people in the recent past. I have collected stories of Red Cliff women who rowed out to Presque Isle, stopping at Wilson Island for a lunch on the way. Another story tells how a few women would row all the way to Bad River to visit relatives.

Such treks would be frowned upon today, partly because of their dangers, but also because of today's expectations of technology. Today only the adventure seeker "paddles or rows" out onto the big lake. Yet these old traditions of Red Cliff Ojibwe using the islands are not dead. Recently, two reservation men used a fourteen foot aluminum boat with an outboard motor to go over to Oak Island to harvest blueberries. And with the continued growth of interest in "traditional ways" on the reservation, we should expect that there will be "a going to the islands" as in the days of old. The stories of women rowing to Bad River and Presque Isle were set in the 1920's and 1930's. That was not so long ago.

Today it seems the Apostle Islands are not usually considered as "Ojibwe Country." Such a label is too often reserved for the land within the actual boundaries of the reservations. But with the recent court decisions regarding the harvesting of resources on ceded lands, the notion of what constitutes Ojibwe Country must be reconsidered. The Apostle Islands are ceded lands.

But Joe Attikoosh recalled more than summers on the islands. He also knew week-long camping trips to the pine barrons west of Washburn, Wisconsin. "The Barrons" were prime blueberry picking country for years, and remain so today. Little "villages" of pickers would suddenly sprout out there, especially in the Depression years of the 1930's. Unemployed people from throughout northwestern Wisconsin came to The Barrons to make needed cash in those years. Red Cliff people had a village as did Ojibwe from the Bad River reserve. Even the Ho-Chunk (then called, by outsiders, the Winnebago) from south-central Wisconsin would sometimes make the long drive up for the blueberry season.

And Joe told of other ventures to bring in some cash. He spent a season cutting aspen ("cutting pulp") in Northern Minnesota. He told me about it, how he toughed it out in the camp far from home. He said it did not like it, and that he took the job because others were doing it and he felt he really needed the money at the time. He said—and this was told to me one afternoon when the two of us were again seated around his little campfire out at Raspberry—that he was up in Minnesota for a few months, getting more and more homesick. "But the woods looked like it does here at Red Cliff, like along this river here, and that kept me going."

Two Red Cliff elders, Rose and John Buffalo, told of a season in The Barrons when they took a hen and its chicks along.

John said, "We drove a small stake into the ground with a long cord tied to it. The other end we tied to one of the hen's legs. She had to stay put and the chicks never wandered far from her." They also told of doing this with a hen on a trip out to Presque Isle. In this case the chickens were all placed into a bushel basket with another inverted over its top. This was safely placed in the middle of the rowboat for the crossing. Even the Ho Chunk from south-central Wisconsin would sometimes make the long drive up for the blueberry season.

Joe knew the love of a woman. A few years after his death a friend of his told how in his younger years Joe had gone down to take as job in the big sawmill on the Menominee Reservation in east-central Wisconsin. The friend, now in his early eighties, told of Joe living with a woman down there, and that there were rumors of a child. This pleases me. It is comforting to think that somehow Joe Attikoosh might be living through this offspring.

Born in the 1920's, Joe was a young man in the years when the local Bureau of Indian Affairs agent was still a person of considerable power on the reservation, a power rivalled only by the resident Catholic priest. Joe saw the beginnings of the end of this old power structure when the federal government passed the Indian Reorganization Act in 1934. This act caused the formation of the first tribal councils at Red Cliff. These elected reservation leaders began to challenge the power of the Indian agent, and thirty years later, in the 1960's, more drastic changes came about that have forever changed things on the reservation. A renewed militancy appeared that, along with other changes across the United States and Canada, has brought a new freedom and responsibility to the Ojibwe.

Joe Attikoosh lived through all this, but seemed unaffected by it. It's not that he was apolitical, because in a very deep sense he was very political. He did not speak to me about politics in the usual way. His politics concerned the land and how a human being could establish a meaningful, perpetually maintaining relationship with it. Joe was one of those people at Red Cliff who walked lightly on the land. This is political in a much more important way than any of the world's national leaders can be political.

Joe was what the anthropologist calls a hunter and gatherer, but as is usually the case, with modifications. While he did work as a wage laborer, this was an overlay, a veneer. To me he was at his best when not working for money. Since he was a person of the northern woods and waters, his politics—and economics—played out less through voting, arguing issues, and picking up a paycheck on Fridays, than simply living in the woods. His politics was like his religion. Both were inseparable from almost everything he did.

In the times he was here Joe was met with the power of the Catholic Church. When I knew him he was not a regular churchgoer, but I have been told he would attend Mass now and then. Never did I attempt to discuss this with him. Such questioning is improper in Ojibwe culture, except in a ritual context. When it came to matters of religion, with Joe I did more listening and watching than questioning.

Like people everywhere, Joe was influenced by the religious beliefs and practices of his parents. His mother is said to have been a strict Catholic. I have heard that his father may have, at times have had his doubts. Be that as it may, strict Catholicism was the vogue at Red Cliff in the early 1900's when Joe was growing up. But just as interesting, the record—both oral and written—tells us that the old Ojibwe religion was still alive in the community in those years. There was a Big Drum. Tent-shaking occurred. The Midewiwin was present. But one is not to write about such things, so the rich details must be left unsaid.

There are a few sugarbush stories that tell something about Joe's religion. Perhaps they can help to fill things in. Once, it is said, he was troubled by a large Grey Owl that visited camp for days on end, each morning and evening. This could have been a bad sign. Its persistent "ko-ko—ko-OO" reverberated through camp just as the crack of sunlight in the morning, waking the men too early. Its evening calls were becoming eerie with the fall of night. As was proper, Joe kept hushed in the owl's presence. Finally, a companion had had enough. One morning, he claims, he "took that rifle, opened the door a crack, pointed the gun up at the big bird, took aim and—plunk—hit him right in the throat. He fell from that tree, dead." This terrified Joe. An owl was not to be harmed.

Another time it was a leaning cedar tree in camp that, in the proper wind, would voice loud, slow creaking sounds. This kept on for some time, worrying him. He spoke about it, but again stayed his distance from the tree. Finally, his more daring companion again took drastic action. As the companion told me, "I took an ax and chopped that damn tree down." Again, Joe was distraught. You do not treat the spirits so casually.

Other tales, less directly speaking to religious matters, still tell of the spirits. There occasionally were times that saw the consumption of too much wine in camp, a practice sure to cause trouble. Once the boiling fire was not tended closely enough and one of the tall hemlocks that held a crossbeam for the kettles caught fire. Its crown was destroyed, killing the tree and showering the open kettles of sap with an inch or more of resinous ash. A companion was on a distant ridge, cutting firewood when he heard Joe shout. He said the tree was a burning beacon in the bright daylight, its flames reaching way up in the sky. Luckily, after the rapid torching of the needles subsided, the fire went out. Joe saw the accident as an omen.

A similar tale told of Joe falling asleep in camp, on the ground, one sunny day as he leaned against a maple tree. He was alone that day and claimed to be wakened by someone gently "rubbing my mouth and chin." He said it was two black bear cubs licking his sweet skin. With his shout they, and their nearby mother ran into the woods. *Makwa,* the black bear, is a very powerful munidoo. It is no little thing to have been so close to it, especially a mother with cubs.

Although Joe lived to see the start of political and religious change in the late 1960's and into the 1970's, he did not witness the "coming out" of some major aspects of traditional religion. In his later years there were some reservation residents who openly stopped attending church, choosing instead the ways of old, but the open ceremonies found in the community today were still to come. Joe's religion was more of a syncretism of Christianity with the old Ojibwe ideologies.

His death came quietly. He had been living in a single roomed wood-frame building in the back yard of a longtime reservation family. He was found dead in his cot. I did not learn of it until a few weeks later when someone phoned our distant city home. The call was for other reasons, but in the conversation my wife was almost casually told that Joe Attikoosh had died. There was a funeral and he was buried in the local cemetery.

My sadness was extreme. I would have wanted to be present at the burial. This was no ordinary man, I felt. I would have wanted to be there to the end.

In his recent little book of his ramblings along the big lake's southern shores, *Northern Passages—Reflections from Lake Superior Country,* the Washburn, Wisconsin, geologist/writer, Michael Van Stappen laments the loss of the large yellow birch forests that were found here long ago. Van Stappen tells how we should become more involved in what he calls "ecological restoration" of the neglected yellow birch as well as its old companions like hemlock and white pine. Such restoration, and the diversity it affords, he claims, is essential to us. This restoration will be difficult, but he says, "it can and should be done. For the yellow birch and for our children and their great-great-grandchildren, it must be done."

I see a poignant parallel between Van Stappen's lament for the yellow birch and my lament for Joe Attikoosh. Has our world become too small for yellow birches and Joe Attikooshes? Joe's relationship to life's forces bigger than he must not be set aside and forgotten. It is not something to be cataloged and placed safely into a cardboard box for storage on a shelf in Madison at the State Historical Society.

Joe Attikoosh forged a conciliation with his world. In the words of William Kittredge, he "was quiet" on the land. In the rich Ojibwe religious cosmology we find a pathway heading to the west. It is burdened with several side roads, all tempting with their enticing allures. Joe may have tried to journey on one or two of these side roads now and then, but he recovered and always found the main trail. I think he was on the right path all along—all through his life. He found the circle at the road's end.

It may be that today no one in the world outside the reservation communities remembers Joe Attikoosh. He might have been one of "those Indians" who walked his life's path, invisible to the outside eye. But perhaps it had to be this way. When he was here there was so much power in the hands of "the Agent and the Priest." Joe did what he could. He kept the old ways alive by living them and, at times, sharing several with some of us. We keep his stories, his ways, alive.

And finally, I want to believe that as a "hunter and gatherer" Joe has shown us that even in today's high-tech world the good way is still possible. Like the yellow birch, he tells of the importance of diversity. As we in the modern world recognize more and more that we are moving in a circle, the teachings of Joe Attikoosh become more and more valuable.

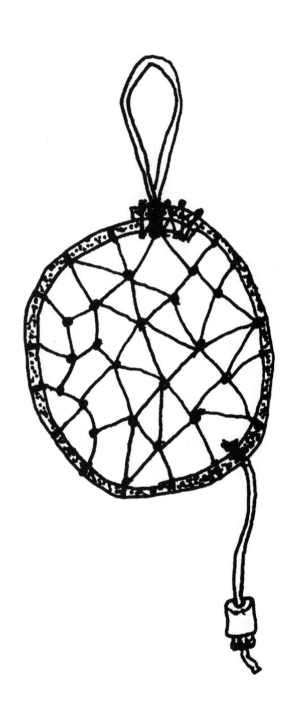

A Woodland Artistry

Veronica sat at her kitchen table, her back to the wall. Mike rested at the table's other side, the one nearest cupboards surrounding the sink. I was in a wooden chair near them closer to the tiny cast iron potbellied stove they use to heat this part of the small house. The heat from the fire was nearly too hot, but no one complained. It was almost twenty below outside.

We waited for the *lug*. Its pleasing aroma filled the room but Veronica said it wasn't done yet.

"Just wait. Patience. You can't rush *lug,*" she told us.

Lug is short for "lugalade," an unleavened bread. In Canada, it is called *bannock*. It is an old-time bread, made long ago at Red Cliff, and kept alive today. Just the mention of lug can bring smiles to some faces. Over the last several decades it has been replaced in many houses by store-bought squishy white bread, and for a generation of youngsters it became a symbol of hard times. "Ma made *lug* when we had nothing else," I was once told.

But in Veronica's kitchen, *lug* does not take a back seat. It never assumed the submissive posture of "poverty food." All her adult life she made it, and always it was made willingly, even with a degree of quiet Ojibwe pride. Veronica is very good at making *lug*, in fact maybe she is the best.

"Hey," I kidded. "I don't think I can wait much longer. I guess I'll make a quick run to the store."

"Gaawiin," Mike said. "Just wait."

At eighty, he was slowing down, suffering from serious diabetes. He was showing problems with walking. In fact, I rarely saw him outside anymore. For a man who lived his life in the woods and on the lake, this was serious. Then there was that back surgery a few years ago. But one of his nicknames is "Ironman." It will take more than diabetes to stop him.

Veronica rose, picked up a soft cloth pot holder, one with a blackened edge telling of fire, and opened the oven door. She reached in gently pressing a finger down onto the pan of bread. I heard a gentle, approving grunt. She lifted the hot metal pan from the oven and closed the door.

She placed the hot pan of golden brown bread onto another hotpad on the table. It rested near the edge, out of reach of Mike.

"Let it cool for awhile," she told us. But in less than a minute Mike jumped up quickly, slid around the table, found a knife and cut himself a generous piece. As he moved back to his chair he was placing a corner of the hot, soft bread into his mouth.

Moments later, Veronica handed me a piece. As I bit into it I closed my eyes and knew it was good. The three of us sat silently eating. For this first piece at least, none of us added anything. The butter would wait for the second piece.

Veronica is an artist with her *lug* baking. She is an artist with great finesse. Like her, other reservation women practice a highly developed art in their kitchens, but at baking lug I think she is the best.

But her art is not seen simply in its finished product. That's too easy. Veronica's artistry involves a lifetime of learning. She learned from her mother, a woman I remember. Veronica interpreted her mother's ability to make lug, and tweaked the baking process here and there. Like all artwork, the bread involves a process. Veronica mastered this process. She added her own polish. She made the recipe hers.

An important part of the definition of art is interpretation. The artist experiences a world and comes to an understanding with it. The world is interpreted. This is shown in the result of artistic effort. And values are involved as well. Cultural values.

Art—according to Vermont anthropologist William Haviland—is the creative use of the human imagination to interpret, understand, and enjoy life. As a child, Veronica stood by while her mother made lug. The girl used her imagination as she developed an understanding of the bread-making process. And in all this she learned to enjoy it. *Lug* has value. Through her *lug,* Veronica values and enjoys life.

And I have watched the artistry of her husband as well. For years I have watched this man at work in the reservation woods. Whether it was skinning out a black bear, carefully trimming a balsam bough for use in maple sap boiling, erecting a log cabin's walls and roof beams, or simply sharpening a double-bit ax, he did so as an artist. It has been a joy, all these years, to be part of this.

No one has a sharper ax than Mike Newago, and I am certain no one handles an ax with the ease, efficiency, joy and artistry as he. At times I would put my ax down and watch him.

He could maneuver a long-handled double-bit ax easily with one hand. There were no wasted swings. Surely this was art.

Today, when we think of the art of the Ojibwe we probably call to mind the beaded floral designs of traditional clothing. These multicolored flowers with dark green leaves, stems, and vines are well known. Bead work on soft black velvet. Bead work on soft, tanned and smoked deer or moose hide.

Secondly, we would probably call to mind the birchbark. Baskets. Canoes. If we have done our homework we might know of the thin pieces of birchbark with designs bitten into them by the artist's teeth.

Then our memories might be on a roll and we recall porcupine quill work and the bulrush mats. Hand woven sashes, sometimes of basswood fiber, sometimes of human or animal hair, and after European contact, woolen yarn will be next. And what about the rock pictographs and petroglyphs? And the midewiwin birchbark scrolls? Pipe stems and soft stone bowls? Porcupine hair roaches?

And then there are the wooden carved tools for granulating maple sugar and for forming the sugar cakes. The hardwood war clubs of long ago and all those lacrosse sticks have aspects of art worked into them.

Most of this is art that was used in a utilitarian way, rather that art made to be hung on a lodge wall and left there. Tribal peoples use their art as they use other objects. Art is not separate from most other parts of their culture. Like their religion, it is woven into practically everything they do. This is how Veronica and Mike do it. Their art is deeply embedded in their lives.

Red Cliff has always had artists. There were painters who, when called upon, would paint designs onto the heads of drums. Betsy Gurnoe was a painter. Walt Bressette painted. And now the best known reserve painter is Rita VanterVenter. Several youngsters are thought to be excellent artists, and in time, they might become better known. But painting in oils or acrylics on one-dimensional media is only one version of art.

Forty years ago it was bead work that was the most popular. A few older women made daisy chains. These seed bead necklaces took their name from the small flower-shaped circles of beads, about one-quarter inch in diameter, that were stitched together into chains. When adding a tiny clasp, they could be fastened around the wrist or neck.

Other beaded items were usually done on a loom. Bracelets, anklets, belts and headbands. But the pieces were always small, almost tentative. It seems that the artists were holding back, uncertain about letting their work pull them out into bigger things. This is the conclusion I drew back then, in the early

1960's. The desire to do bead work was evident, the memories still alive, but there was this hesitancy.

Part of the early stereotype of the American Indian is that they are good with their hands. Maybe this was behind the nineteenth century efforts of Minnesota missionary William Whipple to have native women crochet linen lace. A collection of this fancy handwork rests at the Minnesota Historical Center today. When it was on exhibit a few years ago, I marveled at its beauty and at the thinking of Whipple.

The Indian was good with his hands. Manual things. "Leave the mental things for others" is said to be the not-so-hidden implication. Build industrial training schools. Yes, a few might be able to go on to other things, but for the bulk of them it is better to teach something else. Send them to Carlisle. Colonel Pratt has the answer. Butchers, bakers and candlestick makers—but philosophers? Diplomats? Artists?

When in Indian Country today one is met by murals. These huge, long, colorful, and very powerful wall paintings can be found in casinos, bingo halls, community centers, grade and high schools, tribal colleges, health centers, administrative buildings, and more.

Recently, at the Ojibwe community of Lac Courte Orielles in Northern Wisconsin, I viewed such massive examples of community self-expression. They represent, perhaps, a major change in such expression. Part of a recent florescence, they did not exist fifty years ago. There has been an explosion. Who knows where it will lead? It has only begun.

We are familiar with Indian musicians. This form of art has a long history at Red Cliff. Two years ago when Acorn Gordon, at age 65, sat in the front row at a reservation funeral service for an aunt and he played his guitar while singing a song, I sat quietly with the others. High art. It was beautiful.

In the 1970's when some of the Gordon boys lived in Milwaukee and formed a rock band called the R.C. Express I was awed at their music too. Now and then they came home and put on a concert. Loud, piercing music. Shouting. Angst. Protest music. It was a far cry from the 1920's when Red Cliff men would join with young Bayfield musicians and play their clarinets, trombones, and accordions at town dances. There were no waltzes in the repertoire of the R.C. Express.

In the 1800's, there were fiddlers who played at reserve dances. Square dances mostly, and often held inside houses, these were happy, social affairs that could go into the night. Today the DePerry Family holds an ancient violin going back to those times. While, twenty years ago, a great-granddaughter learned to play it—the Suzuki Method—she has since put it aside. Maybe soon she, or another person in the family line, will pick it up. It seems the time for such a thing.

And there were, and still are, several Red Cliff guitarists. The best known today is Frank Montano, who also plays the woodland flute and other instruments, but a young man in the DePerry line is also a renowned guitarist with at least one compact disc to his credit.

Performance art has always been part of Ojibwe culture. The dancing garb of Robbie Goslin, his wife, and the many others at the annual tribal pow wow continue this tradition. In the distant past, young Ojibwe men used wooden flutes as they sang courtship songs, hoping to win a young woman's hand. This and other forms of creative, spontaneous singing was to be replaced by the practiced performances of Christian hymns.

The "Indian Pageants" of the early twentieth century, although nearly one hundred years ago, involved singing, and the 1954 Red Cliff celebration of the signing of the 1854 treaty—called "The Centennial"—is another example. It was held at Buffalo Bay. This outdoors stage show included the Ojibwe soprano Edna Cloud and Red Cliff's Richard Morris doing their rendition of "Indian Love Call" as they came into the bay by canoe.

Mrs. Cloud was from the Bad River community. Twenty or

so years ago, I finally met her and could not resist asking about her singing. She was pleased to respond, sharing with me her memories of the magic night long ago when she sang with Nelson Eddy in Chicago's Soldier Field. When I met her, Mrs. Cloud was living in the plains Ojibwe community at Turtle Mountain, North Dakota. (We too often might forget that there are Ojibwe communities on the Great Plains.)

The theater continues to be part of Ojibwe life. Roman Catholic Mass, with its rich symbolism and detailed rituals, is a theatrical performance that most Red Cliff residents are familiar with. All the elements of theatre—script, stage, actors, and numerous props—are present. And the more traditional ceremonies are theatrical as well. The purification lodge, shaking tent, and midewiwin lodge are all "stages" on which actors perform. Performance art continues at Red Cliff.

And there is much more that could be said about art at Red Cliff. This past winter when young Joe DePerry and his cousin Kayla DePerry won even more trophies for their expertise in downhill skiing at the local ski hill outside Washburn, they were exhibiting a form of art. When I see these youngsters on the hill I sometimes think of the highly trained and skilled "artists" we see every few years on our TV screens racing down steep snow-covered hills. Is it merely a fine-tuned athleticism, or is it art?

One does not have to think long about this form of joyful expression at Red Cliff. There was a very good Red Cliff baseball team in the 1940's. Today, Red Cliff's Jon DePerry still throws a screaming fastball and shows a wicked, breaking curve ball. His poise on the mound is often commented upon. Athletic art.

Performance art through sports was seen recently when the old game of lacrosse was brought back to Red Cliff.

As an artist, Veronica Newago is not alone at Red Cliff. There is the sewing of Theresa Gordon-Cherette, the paint and birchbark work of Jenny Goslin and Dianne DeFoe. There are the birchbark canoes of Marvin DeFoe and the efforts of all the others working in numerous forms. For years, Delores Bainbridge has brought us the old language and now this linguistic art is being renewed by Mark Gokee, Keller Paap and others.

A cornucopia of art is spilling onto the land. From daisy chains to wall murals, once again, Red Cliff's artists are painting on big canvases, using bold strokes.

Last spring, I stopped at the Newagos' for a visit. The pot-bellied stove was throwing heat as I sat with Veronica and Mike. We sipped hot coffee and talked of things. We nibbled at a few heavily frosted cinnamon rolls I brought from Peterson's Grocery.

"These sure aren't lugalade," I said.

Veronica glanced at me, then replied with a smile, "I was thinking about making some."

Night Forest

Marlene dropped me at the Frog Creek cabin's trailhead. I swung my canvas pack onto my back; a plastic sack of groceries rustled in a hand. Her parting words still echo in my ears: "Be careful!"

The mile-long trail is narrow and winding, the sort of old logging road common on the reservation. The low spots might hold water in the wet times, their clay sucking at my boots. After about a half mile of higher, more level ground, the trail turns thirty degrees to the left and starts its descent to Lake Superior. Although it goes downhill, this last half mile is not precipitous. Except for a single, short, almost steep grade right at its start, the rest is a gradual, comfortable walk, a gentle decline.

There was no moon or starlight last night. A thick cloud cover had lingered all day and I expected rain. The easy wind from the west told of it, even smelled like rain, so I hurried along. The woods were very dark, but I still could make out the walls of trees at my sides as I moved along. Sometimes I was guided along by the string of open sky above me.

Most times I remember to bring my small battery-powered head lamp—a Christmas gift from a son. Its beam bobs with my stride and, when focussed properly, can guide me away from water-filled holes. In spring and throughout early summer, small green frogs leap into them as I pass by, their clear "plunk, plunk, plunk" sounds nice to hear. But with the lamp or not, when I walk at night, it's the trees that hold my attention. They always exude their quiet presence, standing quietly beside me all the way to the cabin.

Over the years, I have often made this nighttime trek. It is glorious when in the time of a new, full moon. Then I sometimes stop to study the woods, looking into its depths, especially when the leaves are down. Sometimes, if I have been careful to be quiet when entering, I can catch the fleeting image of a white-tailed deer leaping away.

On some trips I am startled by a large animal—a deer, I try to assume—bounding through the brush, snapping small branches. A few times my heart pounded from the unexpected burst of a partridge lifting off at my feet. Once it was an owl that startled me as it took wing, then flew low along the trail ahead of me before it turned into the trees and was gone.

The woods in all seasons can be alive at night. Usually, on these trips, I don't dally. If in winter I'm usually on snowshoes and I keep a fast pace, one that warms me, as I anticipate starting a fire in the cabin's stove. In mosquito season I also move quickly, trying to hurry by before they notice and rise to begin their needled attack. At other times, in spring and fall, I'll go more slowly.

A few years ago rumors telling of "panther" sightings circulated on the reserve. "It was black and with that long tail," a cousin said. Then, with the recent assurances from Department of Natural Resources personnel in Minnesota and Wisconsin that cougars were moving back into Lake Superior country, I think about these big cats, especially when on one of my night walks to the cabin.

The taking of backyard pets, and even the loss of a child by mountain hikers out west come to mind. A son and his wife, living in Utah, assure us that these things have happened. But in Wisconsin's north woods? Cougars once were native to this land and with official assurances of their return perhaps we had better pay attention. But would a cougar attack a grown man?

It seems I would be no match for a determined cougar. I carry no gun and usually have no knife, ax, or other weapon.

So—when approaching that mature hemlock where the trail turns at the top of the incline, I tip my head back and let my head lamp's beam scan the big bare branch hanging above at the trail's side. So far it has always been empty. When forgetting to bring the head lamp I push such fears out of my mind, telling myself these woods are safer than city streets.

But there are good reasons for being concerned about walking the woods at night. My wife's command is heeded. Perhaps these concerns give a needed balance to the otherwise carefree and possibly unrealistic joys of the pure wonder of such nocturnal walks. Thoreau does not tell us of any such fears on his many night walks. He appreciated their serenity and wonder. I, too, welcome these gifts but I look and listen for the four-leggeds who live in these woods. This is their home. I only visit now and then.

Last night, upon reaching the cabin and finding it undisturbed, I once again felt the hint of relief that visits me at these times. The mile walk through the dark woods had been as invigorating as ever. I had heard movement in the darkness, some from frightened birds, others from small and larger animals hurrying away, and I was reminded again, that in my absence, life goes on here.

I lit a few oil lamps and in their soft light I hurriedly kindled a fire. The lamp light and the first waves of heat from the barrel stove added to my comfort as I emptied my pack and put the few groceries away. Then, stepping outside to turn on the propane so I could make a small pot of coffee, I checked the winds for any early raindrops. And I studied the sky, hoping for glimpses of starlight indicating that the cloud cover was moving out. Finding none I stepped back into the cabin to settle in for the night and to wait for the rain.

The books tell me that usually The People stayed put at night. With the onset of darkness it was proper to be inside your lodge where you retreated after the day's activity. Generally, unless clearly involved in the food quest, a person out at night, especially someone alone was suspect.

Winter nights were the time to gather for story-telling. Many *manidoog* are said to be asleep, often underground, in the cold season, so in winter it is safe to speak of them. The Vermillion Lake Ojibwe artist Carl Gawboy has rendered an attractive painting of such a lodge scene. He shows an elder telling stories beside a lodge fire, while young and old gather around.

Yet, for some, the night is also a time to be out in the woods or on the water. Spring spearing is done at night, in the old days by birchbark torchlight—hence the name Lac du Flambeau (Lake of the Flaming Torches) for one of Wisconsin's Ojibwe communities. When such spearing was renewed on ceded land in the 1980's in Northern Wisconsin, some nights were loud with the shouts of non-Indian protesters. Now, in 2001, this has quieted and spring spearing has returned to what it was for years and years—an almost silent harvesting of fish.

Fire-hunting also occurs at night. In his autobiography set in the early 1800's in Lake Superior's Ojibwe Country, John Tanner tells of using torches to hunt deer at night. Mike Newago, a Red Cliff resident, tells me he did this kind of hunting on the reservation's waterways. Deer came to the water to drink and eat in the cover of darkness, and he would attach a torch (later a large flashlight) to the bow of a canoe and go out in search of them. Such fire-hunting was common in Ojibwe culture in the past, and it still continues today.

In the days of the popular smelt runs on Lake Superior's south shore, Red Cliff people went to the beaches at night, built large fires and seined the small fish. These were often almost festive events that could last as long as the silvery fish came into the shallows.

There are stories of netting suckers in the reservation's creeks at night. And the late winter spearing that was done through the ice at Frog and Raspberry Bays, even though often done in daylight, still could be said to be a kind of nighttime fishing. The spearer erected a small teepee-like tent over his ice hole and when crawling inside he was in the dark, only the refracted light coming up from the water giving him light.

With the State of Wisconsin's 1897 decision against Red Cliff people fishing the big lake—a decision previously mentioned—the night became, perhaps for most, the time for both fishing and hunting. In fact, for the ensuing 75 years after 1897, most of the taking of game in Red Cliff was accomplished at night. The people adapted. They became expert at this nighttime procurement of food. In many cases, it seems their very existence depended on it.

But the night has not been simply a time for hunting and fishing. It is also a time for ceremonies. The Canadian Ojibwe writer tell of how Wabeno ceremonies typically were nighttime events. The *waabaanowin* is an ancient Ojibwe religious institution that little is written about. A contemporary ethnologist, Thor Conway, claims some Ojibwe religious leaders still practice it. While the better known Ojibwe *midewinin* ceremonies are largely held in daylight—its complex initiation ceremony experiences its high point at noon—the *waabaanowin* ceremonies specialize in nighttime activities, ending with the coming of dawn.

Today, the Ojibwe *jisakaan* (shaking tent) ceremony is held at night. A powerful healing ceremony, it is turned to by the Ojibwe communities in time of need. Today, this ceremony is practiced in numerous Ojibwe locales.

Although it is held during the day, the *madoodiswan* (purification lodge) ceremony has become, usually, a nighttime activity. In his autobiography, *Where the White Man Fears to Tread,* the Lakota activist Russell Means chastises us for using the term "sweat lodge" for this ceremony. He reminds us that it is a religious purification rite and the word "sweat" can carry derogatory connotations. The image of naked, or nearly naked, men (and women) huddled inside a small, dark lodge might appear unseemly to the more "sophisticated" outside eye. Perhaps our association of unpleasant odors with human sweat is at play here. (The Finnish sauna and the hot baths of Japan are not referred to as "sweat ceremonies," although the act of sweating is what they are all about.)

The purification lodge has come back into great popularity in Indian Country. Not simply a matter of erecting a small hut and sitting in the dark enclosure around intensely heated stones, this ceremony can have many ritual obligations. A purification rite such as this is not undertaken lightly.

When inside such a lodge it is easy for me to let my mind flow with the ritual. At the most abstract level such a lodge becomes the cosmos. All the spiritual forces are called inside and, according to some interpretations, the world as we know it is reduced to nothing. The realities we encounter daily are extinguished, then rebuilt. It is a ritual of rebirth. Time and space are no more, as those inside the lodge reenact the world's coming into being. Any way it is approached it is complex and serious.

A purification lodge ceremony uses the ideas of darkness and light to carry out its messages. Time spent inside such a lodge is a time facing the uncertainties of "a night." At the end of the ceremony, when the lodge flap is opened and cool, fresh air rushes in, you are brought to a new time, a new "dawn." You are spiritually made anew. The midewiwin, for example, was said to have had to "go underground" to stay alive. Most of these ceremonies are done discreetly today, out of the public's eye.

And fireballs can be seen at night. To a believer, these fearful sightings tell of a person up to no good. Medicine people from distant villages are suspected of causing these. They are sent out to do harm.

Bear walking also occurs at night. Here a person transforms him or herself into a bear—or another large animal—and goes out to do mischief. In the Ojibwe belief system such examples of transformation are legend. And, of course, at Red Cliff, as at the other reserves, missionaries worked hard to discredit them. The literature tells how the "black coats" competed with tribal religious leaders.

The Episcopal missionary Joseph Gilfillan, who worked in Minnesota Ojibwe communities in the 1800's, wrote a novel based on this theme. As sometimes seen in missionary literature written today, at the end the last holdout of "savagery," the village religious leader, converts to Christianity.

But over the years the night at Red Cliff was also a time for much lighter activities. People visited each other's homes at night. Children sometimes played outside in the darkness into the evening hours. Night was a time of warmth, but always with the admonition not to go to far into its depths.

When I first came to the village forty years ago, only a single house had electricity. This meant that most homes had no inside plumbing—no running water or flushing toilets. Heat was by fuel oil or wood. Refrigeration was also almost completely absent. Today, in hindsight, this might seem to have made life very difficult. But some of the warmest stories, many taking place at night, come from these times. People remember the strings of oil lanterns moving to a social gathering. "They glowed and swung at times, in gentle arcs with the person's stride. It was something to see."

With the coming of electricity to most of the community came street lights that burn all night. Some families opt for a backyard "security light," a tall utility pole with a light that illuminates the yard until dawn. With such "improvements" the charm of night is pushed away. Now oil lanterns are a rarity at Red Cliff. They have been relegated to the status of antiques.

And the ubiquitous television has changed the night as well. It seems that little visiting is done anymore. When it does occur, as in my extended family of in-laws, it seems as if it is a throwback to something from the past. Now television, videos, and for the younger folk, video games, are popular.

And at Red Cliff, the bingo hall, casino and liquor lounge—a three-in-one recreational complex the tribe erected several years ago, has become the social gathering place. Even tribal council meetings are now held in the bingo hall.

For some reservation residents the night might have lost some of its allure. Several years ago I was determined that the full moon over Raspberry Bay would not be missed. I and an adult daughter insisted that her mother and grandmother had to join us on an overnight campout on the big beach. After much work they grudgingly agreed to come along. We found a younger niece who was eager to be part of the party. So one Friday evening just at dusk we drove out to the empty campground and walked the long boardwalk through the bog to the beach. There were five of us, plus my daughter's huge black labrador.

The niece and daughter kindled a small fire as I set up the tent we intended to sleep in. The huge moon, a light orange color, was right before us out on the lake, over the islands. I had hopes of all of us sitting around the fire late into the night with food, drink, and unending stories. But it did not happen. Almost as soon as the tent was set up, right when darkness settled in, my wife and her mother announced they were "going to bed." They crawled into the tent and did not come out until daylight.

The rest of us stayed with the fire into the night and enjoyed it. We finally fell to sleep beside the fire, wrapped in blankets. There were no mosquitos or other pests. The dog slept well.

Later, I was chastised by a member of the tribe for taking those women out to the beach at night. Unknown to me, it was a time of setting and lifting fishnets at a location on the beach quite distant from our campsite and the man referred to the possibility of bears coming in at night for the fish. I still wonder about this reprimand.

Maybe a few rough fish were found in the nets and then tossed aside on the beach. Maybe hungry bears did come in for them. Maybe there was a danger. But I think there was more at play here. Today, a Red Cliff woman is rarely in the woods. And certainly a lonely, isolated beach at night is perceived as no place for a grandmother to be sleeping in a tent. I think of how things have changed. In the past women were deeply involved in the matters of fishing, gathering, trapping and even, at times, hunting. Both the spring sugarbush and fall rice camp are said to have been the domain of the woman.

But there might also be something else at play in my male friend's remark. Perhaps it shows that an isolated night beach is not really a place to sit and contemplate the moon. The big lake is a power much bigger than us. It is where the people go for sustenance. It is not something to be looked at for esthetic reasons only. Ojibwe don't sit and ponder the wonder of nature. Instead they accept its wonder and power, and in this act supplicate themselves to it. Maybe a beach like Raspberry, especially at night, is like the cemetery. It is a place to be left alone.

Throughout the world's cultures, the beach is, like all important boundaries, said to be a sacred place. It stands structurally, between water and land. It mystically is both, while it is neither. It is betwixt and between. It can be a place of befuddling uncertainty, but also a place of penetrating clarity. This sort of thinking was behind my desire to spend that warm, wonderful night on Raspberry Beach, but we sometimes discover that such places can be perceived differently by different people. Culture makes a difference.

The symbolism of day and night is ancient. Perhaps its depths of meaning are internal, even in non-human forms of life, triggered by mechanical factors, driven by DNA with its finite triads of chemicals. Plants reach for the day, turn to the light. Some fold up, like many animals, to "sleep" at night. Their time is a time of daylight. Night is a metaphor for death, day for life. We speak of having your "time in the sun." Shakespeare wrote of a winter of discontent, a time of uneasiness, a time of darkness.

If we humans fear darkness we are far different from our non-human fellows who are nocturnal, who come alive at night. These colleagues feed at night and rest, even sleep in daylight. Much of this is said to be for survival. Deer generally are active at night.

This is what my nights in the sugarbush and Frog Creek cabins do for me. Renewal. When the mice problem is not extreme, the cabin can be quiet at night. The gentle murmur from the woodburning stoves is welcome on winter nights. As I lie in bed the light of the fire that escapes through the stove doors' open dampers sometimes bounces around the cabin walls. And when I am in the darkened cabins, in bed, the welcome patter of raindrops is sometimes heard. It is another welcome night sound.

Then there are the songs of the marsh wren and the sedge wren. The marsh wren often sings at night while the sedge wren also does, but less often. A night-singing bird! While still uncertain which I hear—or is it both?—I have heard nighttime wren song each spring and summer at Frog Creek. I marvel at these tiny, brown birds! Why do they sing when all the others are silent? Science's utilitarian answer—bird song is about territory and mating—does not do it for me anymore. I conclude that these wrens, too, find joy in the night and that they choose to sing about it.

These birds, like all the others we share these woods with, are our neighbors, but still are strangers. They come to the land as we do, but we do not speak their language, nor they ours. All we can do is watch them, and listen. But in their song they tell us nothing. The birds do not sing for us. We infer a message, try to make some sense of their behavior. Perhaps there finally is no message. They simply go about their business—mating, rearing their young, and always, searching for food. Reproduction and economics again. How clear it seems to be. For them it might be enough. Yet, I like to think that the wren's singing in the night might be like our dancing in the rain. Maybe sometimes the night and the rain are simply too much to just let be. Maybe the birds, and some humans who care to, celebrate them. I like to think so.

On the best of cabin nights when I have become drowsy from reading and writing, I sometimes step outside to be freshened by the cool night air, or simply to drain my full bladder. At such times, I often stand for a few extra moments just to view the cabin. The Frog Creek cabin has a row of tall windows that I like to see lit up at night. The deep yellow glow of the oil lamp floods out into the woods, calling to mind a Terry Redlin print. Once, on such a night, I set up my camera's tripod and attempted to capture the soft, golden image.

And then there is the aurora borealis. The northern lights can be spectacular at Red Cliff. At Frog Creek, the thick woods can restrict the view, but if I take the time to hike the quarter mile out to the beach, or if I am adventuresome enough to take the canoe out on the lagoon, the thrill is worth it. Legends tell that the moving lights are the spirits of the deceased, but there are many such worldwide explanations. What is comforting is that even today the scientific community still cannot explain their specifics. It is said they are formed by flares, or energy blasts, released from the sun that collide with the earth's atmosphere, causing the lights at the poles. But just why we see the color and spectacular movement instead of simply a steady glow is unknown. It is comforting to know that there are still mysteries in this world.

But not all cabin nights are so warm and cozy. Once, when stepping out into the darkness, I was startled to hear a large animal behind the cabin. It issued a series of grunts or snorts— a male deer in rut? — and then a series of what I took to be foot stompings. Clearly a posture of threat, it told me I was infringing on its territory.

Some cabin visitors tell of being wakened by bears. Once a son and companion were wakened in the early darkness by what turned out to be a huge black bear. It came up to the cabin from the lagoon, making ample noise in the process, then slowly walked around the cabin before heading out on the trail. They put a flashlight beam on it and were awed by the animal's size.

And I think of wolves. Timber wolves are said to be back in the area, but I have never sighted any. They must be busy at night. The thrill of a sighting is something I look forward to.

Some versions of Ojibwe origin teachings tell of the beginnings when The People were *manidoog* just like all the other life forms. Since they were spirits, they lived forever. Then *Wenabozo,* who walked over the entire surface of the earth, concluded that this would lead to disaster because the earth's surface was finite. It had only so much room, and since humans kept reproducing themselves, and never died, they would eventually run out of space. To solve this problem, he gave death to The People. (Sometimes the coming of death is explained by the introduction of sleep. At the beginning the people did not sleep. In this teaching, we see sleep used as a metaphor for death.) This paradox, the introduction of death to bring life, is common in world origin statements.

Some Ojibwe stories tell of other early medicine people who were involved in the process of creation. There could be contests of power in which a religious leader would attempt to control the coming of the sun at dawn. Sometimes such a person was able to keep the sun from rising, thus causing an ongoing, never-ending night. Always this is corrected by letting the sun, finally, rise to start a new day.

We see in such statements that the early people were involved in truly cosmic questions. Ojibwe religious teachings have many stories that deal with cosmology and cosmogony—with the universe and its beginnings. What is finally affected in these statements is an acceptable balance between things, especially between the sun and moon, the waters, skies, and the earth, and also between life and death. This includes a necessary balance between day and night.

In the *Manidoo World,* things are in balance. This is simply their nature. Power flows between the spirits and the people, and in this flow the balance is maintained. But in the old view, it is always the spirits that are the most powerful. The people defer to them. Offerings must be made. These sacrifices are a necessary aspect of religious ceremonies.

When everything is in balance the world moves smoothly.

Life and death come and go, like the sun and moon, summer and winter, and like day and night. In such a world the night holds both joy and fear. The people generally rest at night but they can choose, for example, to go to the night to hunt or fish. When doing this they face its fears and uncertainties. But at these times they did so willingly and they know the circumstances. They understand what is expected of them. They take the necessary precautions.

Then came The Change. The Europeans arrived bearing a new kind of power. Their technologies, embedded in a new belief system, affected the way The People lived. There were new laws about sustenance, about the procurement of food, and about relating to the land. The ways of hunting, gathering, and fishing were changed. People had to turn to the night differently, under a certain duress, to survive. For some, the night's joys and fearful uncertainties began to tilt out of balance. And there was more.

Electricity changed the night. In some ways it was washed away with this new light. Perhaps its darkness was denied. And with the change in night had to come a change in its counterpart: day. Both night and day became different to The People, in some extreme cases perhaps, became virtually unknowable. This time "out of balance" dragged on and on.

But finally, things started to change. The new technologies and beliefs began to be altered and accommodated to. Some new things were rejected, others modified. Some people began to listen to the elders more than ever before. New leaders emerged. New elders appeared. Old ceremonies took on new meanings. The Language started to be important again. A new balance started to form. The People and their *manidoog* started "to take back the night."

Inside the cabin I wake to warm morning light. The night winds, with their wonderful smell of rain, fooled me. While I slept the clouds passed, their rain falling elsewhere. The cabin is cool, and I will soon rise to quickly get the stove's fire going again. But first I will lie in this cot, enjoying the view out the cabin's windows. Spring warblers are offering their rippling, melodious songs and a few robins are loud. Moments ago a single deep croak of a raven was heard as the big black bird swept overhead. Then suddenly the dark shadow of a huge bird crosses the trees outside the window and I sit up just in time to see an eagle, its white head bright as a beacon, glide down to the lagoon and reach for a fish. It rises with empty feet and flies out to the lake. Like the bird, I am hungry, so I swing out of bed to make a morning fire. As I pull on my faded blue jeans I think about what I will cook for breakfast.

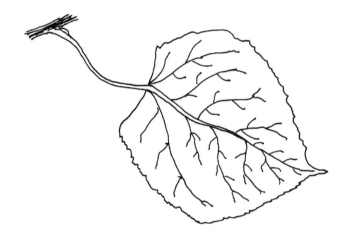

A Shoreline Dream

Good land was a paradise
—Wub-E-Ke-Niero, 1995

It rained earlier this morning. The drops' patter woke me just before dawn, but I quickly went back to sleep. The dream was too good to leave, so I turned over and fell back into it.

We were here at the cabin, Frog Creek Lagoon. It was the year 2001. The family was here—Marlene, all three of our children, our son-in-law, our two daughters-in-law and our four grandchildren. Even the dogs were with us—all three of the wonderful Labradors: one yellow, one chocolate, one black.

And it was more than family. Others were with us—Red Cliff people. They were in this cabin. Thirty or more. Somehow there was room for everyone. A kind of meeting was going on, a council meeting, perhaps. People spoke of things, issues, and they took their time. There was much listening—the good, genuine kind.

We had food. Someone, perhaps it was a few of the nieces and nephews, or else those interesting friends of our youngest son, had dug a pit and roasted a few birds—big ones, turkeys or maybe geese. I'm not sure which. There was mashed potatoes, *jissan* (rutabaga), wild rice. And soup. A large kettle of macroni soup. I saw a raspberry pie.

So with all the talk there was this food, the good smells and tastes. And tea. We were drinking balsam tea. No soda pop. No Pepsi was in sight. Beer was out of the question.

I remember that an older man, grey, thin, and with an air of dignity was speaking. He was articulate. It must have been Alex Roye. He—as did everyone in the dream—spoke quietly but firmly. Something was up. Roads, land, an old drum. Sovereignly—words I remember hearing here and there. There were maps on the cabins walls, colorful ones, shaped like fingernails beside a big lake. Once he spoke at length while holding up an old object of some sort, maybe a dancing stick of some sort. I don't know what it was.

Then the speaker was joined by a woman who had a lot of that newfangled projection equipment. She clicked a hand-held button and we saw image after image on a large screen. CD Roms maybe. Old faces of people who have died. Black and whites, not grainy like old pictures can become, but new-looking. Restored. Buffalo was there, and that missionary, Baraga. More maps with red, white, and green squares and rectangles. Always the rectangles. And the boundaries. The fingernail's outline was clearly marked.

This woman, much younger than the old man, had dark hair and spoke clearly, firmly. She was received approvingly, with respect.

I don't know how we ran all that equipment. There is no electricity out here at the cabin, unless we brought in our little generator. But I did not have a generator running. It was all so quiet. Just the talking and listening, the chewing and tea sipping. It was all so very positive.

But we were not alone. Off in a side room (our little cabin had grown in size) was a gathering of *chimokemaanug* (white people). Most, it seemed, were standing, facing the Ojibwe in the meeting. These whites were quiet, clearly in a state of submission, actually a condition of deferral to the tribesmen. It was as if these white people had had their time in the sun. Now they had to wait for the tribe to conclude its deliberations. It was as if the whites knew the outcome. They were schoolchildren, waiting to be dismissed.

Then the kingfisher woke me. She, or he, was splashing into

the creek after fish again, and as the bird always does, it shot up from the water to perch in a creekside tree, all the while chattering in that loud, wonderful, rapid-fire, in-your-face kingfisher way.

By then the rain had passed. We had sunshine. I lay in the cot and felt for the clock on the floor. It was 6:45 A.M.

So I'm in the woods again. Away from the city. Another weekend at Red Cliff. Frog Bay. It's late spring, past sugarbush time, and before the bugs. This is a good time to be in the woods. No bugs and the greenup is only starting. You can see through the walls of trees. It's open. A time of great clarity.

I decide to fry-up some bacon, eggs, and potatoes. I'll cut an onion in with the potatoes, a whole onion. And this morning it's coffee, thick and deep. Not Starbucks or Caribou, but just as good. My cabin coffee is a mixture of whatever family and friends bring out here. They leave remnant packages of exotic, upscale brands from the city. I dump it all into an old three pound tin of ARCO and stir it. There is still as lot of ARCO in there, so I don't know what it is anymore all mixed up like that. But it perks up into a nice dark, rich, and strong brew. The buzz lasts for a while.

During my first years in these shoreline woods I didn't need the coffee. Just being here gave me a buzz. I was so attached to it, my passion was deep. Its isolation charmed me. I was like the old Finnish sage, Vainamoinen. I dealt with magical potions, mystical charms. My bag of tricks, my *gebic* bag was filled with these trees, this shoreline, this place. They were my magic. I had no sacred harp like Vainamoinen, made from the jawbone of a pike and strung with hairs from the tail of the Demon's steed. The music I made was not as good as his. But I still sang a lot and sometimes I whistled.

All the years I worked on this cabin—it was built, believe it or not, over a period of nearly twenty years—I was in awe of these woods. My campus friends must have tired of my talk: cabin, cabin, cabin. Sometimes, when I look back at those years,

I suspect I would have died for this place. These beaches, those
wild flowers—the boxes and boxes of photos. All that zeal. I
was a missionary.

It's different now. The dream shows me that. The people
were talking quietly. It's not that they were dispassionate about
what they were speaking of—whatever it was—but that their
understanding and commitment was beyond passion. They had
worked through all the foolishness. Now the power was in their
hands. They knew this, and it calmed them, gave them assur-
ance and determination.

It has been said that our passions can become our prisons.
Woods, wilderness like this for example, if held too tightly, can
become a city. You end up with the opposite of what you wanted.
Your extreme attachment to the treasured thing precludes your
defense of it. You're so high, giddy, that you can't function well.
You don't know what a defense is. You are no use as a fighter.

Those dream people were attached. That was a given. It was
clear beyond clear. No one said it, but you knew it was there.
Solidly. Whatever it was they were talking about, it was a passion of theirs. The meeting reeked of passion.

But it was so calm. They spoke so quietly. That young woman
showed picture after picture, map after map, chart after chart.
She had statistics. Numbers. And nothing bored the people.
They were hungry for them. The cabin was charged with their
energy but everything was lined up, balanced out. There was
power in the cabin. Big power.

Those dream people were attached but not attached. Figure
that out. They were steadfast. They lived at the end of a road.
They were staying put, no matter what. This woods was their
home. They loved it, and each other, but no one said this. No
one wrote it down. Maybe no one even thought it. But it was
all over the place.

After my heavy breakfast, I washed up the dishes, made the
bed, and swept the cabin's floor. Then I sat for awhile with

coffee and a sack of small, tongue-biting ginger snaps. I looked through the front windows, down the quarter-mile length of the lagoon, all the way to the islands. I felt like I wanted to push off, paddle out for a summer, maybe even into late fall.

Then, stepping outside for an armful of firewood, I paused to inspect the ground beneath the hemlock tree where the wood is stacked. No golden thread yet. It's too early. The ground must still be cold. Coming back into the cabin with the wood, I lay it down beside the stove. Then the cabin was cleaned up, firewood was brought in. It was time for a hike out to the beach for a better look at those islands.

Several years ago when Carter Rivard, the Osage writer, went to England and the European continent, he stepped ashore and raised both arms, spreading them open and claimed all the land he saw—"vast stretches"— for the Great Sovereign Osage Nation.

How should we respond to this act? Do we chuckle in its humor? Or, as Rivard hoped, at least as I want to think he did, do we hark back to the foolishness of those who came to the Americas and did such claiming not so long ago? History tells us that their claiming was done in all sincerity, sealed with oaths to their gods. Why does Carter Rivard's similar act bring a smile?

The Osage Nation was, in the early 1900's, said to be the richest tribe in the United States. This I learned in grade school back in the early 1940's. Oklahoma oil. The Osage people also suffered a tragic spate of murder, fraud, and theft as enterprising intruders came amongst them to take that black gold. This rape and pillaging remains one of this country's forgotten international tragedies.

When Carter Rivard stood on the deck of a boat coming into a European harbor and announced his claim to all the land he could see, and to miles and miles that he could not see, he had no power. He could not back up his claim with a determined force. Is that where the humor lies? Power and force? The European claimants were backed up with monarchies holding huge armies and navies. Military force.

Does it come down to power and force again?

These Lake Superior woods are powerful. This pristine shore-line exudes power. The relatively undeveloped islands sitting in this deep, cold lake all have it. This morning's eagle, with his strong, outstretched talons grasping for that elusive brook trout, has power. (The fish had power as well as it streaked out of reach.) The *makwag* that use this cabin for a scratching post have it. And those cougars and wolves. Even the coyotes that run through these woods.

And the winters have power. Their cold can reach through me. If I don't prepare for it, don't cut enough wood, don't keep the cabin's walls chinked, in the snowy time the cold could drive me out of here.

Power can be defined as having the ability to cause others to make decisions you want them to make. It is said to stem from having a superior access to valued resources.

Those dream-people knew all this. They were dealing with matters of power. They talked of it. That woman's pictures, maps, and charts showed it.

Today many travelers come to The Rez. Once again America is on the move. It happened a hundred years ago with people "touring" to Red Cliff Creek for the Indian Pageants. It happened in the early post-Civil War years when the recently widowed Mrs. Lincoln and General Sherman toured to Bayfield. President Coolidge came in the 1920's for a shore lunch on one of the islands.

Now it's happening again. Folks of America's Cup vintage are here, and those of the woodsman chic style (caribiners for key-holders) are travelling here now. (If you have never been to the peaks of Patagonia at least you can look like you have!)

Hay fever sufferers came to the Bayfield peninsula "for the air" a hundred years ago. Now holistic health seekers are looking us over—wanting to build retreats on The Rez, one with a modern purification lodge.

Fifty years ago, we in the heartland were admonished to pull up our roots and move to New York or L.A. But it didn't matter where you went, just so you left home. No grass was to grow under your feet. Many of us left home, going to college, sometimes among the first in our family line to do so. We were applauded, sometimes with bittersweet tears, by our stay-at-home parents.

Technology spurred this movement on. First the railroads, then the automobile and airplanes. Route 66. Highway 2. We went to where the action was. But the sort of traveling to The Northland today is of another kind. Now, it seems to me, we are told to travel to places where people have stayed put. The Irish countryside, an Amazon village, a rural Italian town where goat-herders come to market on Tuesdays. Red Cliff's shoreline and the islands.

We have become a country in motion. America on the move. There is so much movement today. We have worked through the years of future shock, only to reach another sort of never-never land.

We travel great distances to get to the Irish countryside, an Alaskan Innuit village, a mountainous Italian hamlet's shoreline and the islands.

Importantly, those of us in the mainstream might need these worldwide places from which the people have never left. Unfortunately, our very coming changes these wondrous places. Our presence can destroy them. Surely, if they desire, these places, these communities, can determine their own destiny. They have a right to exist.